FANTASY
SEX

FANTASY SEX

Flic Everett

Illustrated by Alan Adler

MQP

Contents

The Importance of Fantasy **6**

Men's Fantasies **66**

Women's Fantasies **130**

Talking About Fantasies **194**

Role-play **242**

Alternative Fantasy **290**

Inspiration and Reality **354**

Thoughts on Fantasy Sex **418**

1 THE IMPORTANCE OF **FANTASY**

SEXUAL FANTASY IS THE DIFFERENCE BETWEEN OK SEX AND GREAT SEX.

Fantasizing also keeps you sexually stimulated, even when you have little chance of actually having sex. Whether you're day-dreaming, masturbating, story-telling, or role-playing to spice up your sex life, fantasy provides you with every possible scenario that could ever turn you on.

The brain is your greatest sexual organ, and if you aren't turned on mentally during sex, then physically you'll have a worse than average time. Your mental excitement can transform an average person into a sex god, or goddess, and your bedroom into a sultan's tent filled with petals, a slave ship, or the scene of a black mass. The choice is yours.

Talking about your fantasies opens up your sexuality to your partner, allowing them a vital insight into what turns you on, and why. Even if you don't want to confess all, you can still make suggestions based on your sexual imagination.

CASE STUDY

"A FANTASY IS A PLACE WHERE I CAN HAVE THE
MOST INCREDIBLE SEXUAL THOUGHTS—THINGS I'D
NEVER TELL ANOTHER PERSON—WITHOUT FEELING
ANY GUILT. I JUST ENTER MY OWN WORLD, AND MY
FAVORITE, FILTHIEST FANTASIES ARE ALWAYS THERE,
AND CAN BE ADDED TO ANY TIME. I FANTASIZE
ABOUT EVERYTHING, FROM A SEXY COLLEGE
TUTOR TAKING ME OVER A TABLE OR STRIPPING
ONSTAGE, TO SEX WITH TWO MEN, OR EVEN
THREE. I WOULDN'T DO IT IN REAL LIFE, BUT IN MY
IMAGINATION IT DRIVES ME WILD."

Gemma, 28, Lawyer

The sources of sexual fantasy are infinitely varied, but they often stem from the time when your sexuality was awakened—through books you read, places you visited, or movies you saw. The images that became erotic to you then may still have the same effect, but they will be honed and developed over time.

A FANTASY CAN BE AS SIMPLE AS
IMAGINING YOU'RE OUTDOORS IN SUMMER,
WHEN IN REALITY, YOU'RE IN BED
AND IT'S WINTER; OR, IT CAN BE AS
COMPLEX AS GROUP SEX WITH A THOUSAND
ROMAN SLAVES. YOU CAN INDULGE
YOUR EVERY WHIM....

STORY

Captured by pirates, a woman is tied to the ship's mast. The pirate captain moves nearer to her as the sea crashes over the deck. While his men watch, he removes his sword and, with the very tip of it, slices off her thin dress. The dress falls away to reveal that she's naked beneath. The ship's men are all driven mad with lust at the sight of her, and fight over who will have her first. The woman, desperate to escape, writhes under the ropes, but she is secretly turned on by the idea of these rough, strong men desiring her body.

However conservative your sex life, it's unlikely that you haven't fantasized either during masturbation or intercourse. Almost all surveys on the subject have revealed that men and women use fantasy to enhance their sex lives, increasing their focus on what's happening during sex or masturbation. Fantasy helps many to concentrate on and enhance the feelings that they're experiencing.

FANTASY BRINGS ANOTHER DIMENSION TO SEX BY
COMPENSATING FOR STIMULI THAT ARE ABSENT IN
REAL LIFE. MORE IMPORTANTLY, IT ALSO ALLOWS FOR
DIFFERENCES IN THE AROUSAL LEVELS OF A COUPLE.
HE MAY BE THINKING "HUGE BREASTS!" WHILE SHE'S
THINKING "BRAD PITT!," BECAUSE BOTH PARTNERS
HAVE DIFFERENT MENTAL FOCUSES—WHICH IS OK,
AS LONG AS YOU'RE BOTH HAPPY.

YOUR SEX LIFE CAN BE IMPROVED BY FANTASY
BECAUSE YOU CAN ILLUSTRATE WHAT TURNS YOU
ON, WHAT WORKS FOR YOU, AND WHAT YOU'RE
SEXUALLY CAPABLE OF. REALIZING THAT YOU'VE
ALWAYS WANTED TO BE A RAUNCHY NURSE, OR
SHARING YOUR EXHIBITIONIST FANTASY OF
OUTDOOR SEX IN THE HILLS, CAN PAVE THE WAY FOR
SOME EXCITING ROLE-PLAYING EXPERIENCES.

CASE STUDY

"I HAVE A FANTASY THAT ALWAYS GETS ME VERY TURNED ON. I'M UNDRESSING IN FRONT OF A WINDOW, AND THIS GIRL PASSES AND LOOKS UP. I SEE HER AND REVEAL MY ERECT PENIS TO HER, THEN I START TO RUB IT WHILE SHE WATCHES. SHE GETS VERY EXCITED WATCHING ME, AND STARTS TO UNDRESS, STANDING IN THE STREET. IT ENDS WITH US BOTH MASTURBATING, WATCHING EACH OTHER, AND COMING TOGETHER. I LOVE FANTASY BECAUSE IT MEANS I CAN HAVE INCREDIBLE ORGASMS ON MY OWN. I THINK I HAVE EXHIBITIONIST TENDENCIES BUT I COULD NEVER EXPOSE MYSELF IN REALITY."

Alex, 38, Chef

In a fantasy you can try things you'd never normally consider—it might be something that in reality you would feel horrified at doing. Shy people might strip, powerful people might be submissive, and unassertive people might dominate others with whips and chains.

STORY

A man stands in a dark room, wearing tight leather trousers, and with his chest bare. To remain anonymous he wears a mask. A woman enters, naked except for high heels; she's come to be punished. She bends forward slightly to receive her punishment, and the man strokes a whip very lightly over her buttocks. He flicks the whip, and the woman gives an impulsive cry of excitement. She turns and starts to rub the man's penis through the leather, before they begin to have vicious sex: biting, pulling each other's hair, and hurting each other. The man and the woman use force to get what they want, pinning or tying each other down. They orgasm in an eruption of screaming and scratching.

THE ONLY LIMIT TO YOUR FANTASY
IS YOUR IMAGINATION, SO IT'S
WORTH RUNNING THROUGH
VARIOUS SCENARIOS—FROM
BOOKS, FILMS, ETC.—AND
STOPPING EVERY TIME YOU
COME UPON AN IDEA THAT
CAUSES SEXY STIRRINGS WITHIN
YOU, EVEN IF IT'S SOMETHING
YOU'VE NEVER CONSIDERED BEFORE.

In a fantasy you can imagine that you are whoever you want to be, and look however you want to. You might be young or old, blonde- or dark-haired, tall or short, male or female—it's entirely up to you, so long as it's really making you hot.

MASTURBATING WITHOUT FANTASY IS A DULL
AND UNSATISFYING EXPERIENCE IF THERE'S
NO MENTAL FOCUS. MEN CAN GET HOT
WITH VISUAL STIMULATION, BUT WOMEN
OFTEN PREFER A MENTAL IMAGE TO
CONCENTRATE ON—WHETHER IT'S SIMPLY A
PICTURE OF A PENIS OR A HOLLYWOOD
PRODUCTION WITH A CAST OF THOUSANDS.

STORY

If you're a woman, imagine how powerful it must be to be a man seducing a woman. Focus on what it must be like to have a penis—the sensation of being able to enter someone else's body and feel the most sensitive part of you enclosed by warmth and wetness. Don't think about who you're with but concentrate on the sensation of pushing your penis in and out, how hard and firm it is. Feel how smooth and springy and erect the penis is. Imagine how it would feel held tightly by a hand, or sucked.

Masturbation fantasies can be based simply on being with a partner, particularly if you're single, or, as is more frequently imagined, on being with someone who isn't your usual partner. Usually these fantasies are fairly quick, simple, and effective.

Celebrities are often a favorite image for masturbation fantasies, since they present a glamorous, ideal image of perfection. Sometimes the turn-on of imagining being chosen by somebody perfect can be important too. The idea that this someone —who could have anyone—might pick you is extremely arousing in itself.

Fantasy can boost your self-esteem.
If you imagine yourself as young,
beautiful, or infinitely desirable, your
sexual responses are heightened
because you aren't hampered, as you
are in a real sexual scenario, by
wondering if the girth of your penis is
great enough or if your bum's too big.

CASE STUDY

"FANTASIZING INCREASES MY SELF-ESTEEM. I'M A
LITTLE OVERWEIGHT AND FAIRLY ORDINARY, BUT
IN MY FANTASIES EVERYBODY WANTS ME. I
DANCE ON A BAR, SHOWING MYSELF OFF,
OR I MAKE LOVE WITH ONE MAN WHILE
OTHERS LINE UP TO HAVE A TURN. AFTER I'VE
MASTURBATED I FIND I FEEL GOOD ABOUT
MYSELF FOR QUITE A WHILE—IT'S AS THOUGH
WHEN I FANTASIZE I CAN SEE HOW SEXY I
COULD BE IF I DIDN'T FEEL SO INHIBITED ABOUT MY
BODY. IT'S IMPROVED MY SEX LIFE—MY BOYFRIEND
WAS REALLY TURNED ON WHEN I TOLD HIM."

Jayne, 35, Manager

FANTASY IS BEST WHEN YOU CHOOSE YOUR SCENE BEFORE YOU BEGIN SEXUAL PLAY. RUNNING THROUGH A RANGE OF OPTIONS CAN LEAD TO CONFUSION AND DISTRACTION, WHICH IS NOT HELPFUL IF YOU'RE CLOSE TO CLIMAX AND YOUR FANTASY ISN'T WORKING OUT.

Many people have a mental list of their favorite fantasies. The basic ideas that turn them on in the fantasy remain the same—whether it's a raunchy schoolgirl or a sacrificial virgin, or merely being the proud owner of enormous breasts—and are modified or developed accordingly.

Most fantasy is not harmful but simply enhances the basic sexual experience, whether during masturbation or partnered sex. There are several common fantasies dealing with themes that are arousing because they revolve around something that's desirable but impossible in real life.

Movie Sex

WHEN YOU FANTASIZE ABOUT A MOVIE
STAR, YOU CAN "HAVE SEX" WITH ANY
CHARACTER OF YOUR CHOICE, FROM
HUMPHREY BOGART TO HANNIBAL LECTER.

Movie sex scenes also provide a basis for fantasy since they usually take place in interesting locations, such as in the back of a limousine, or on a kitchen table. We may not want or be able to re-enact them in reality, but they provide extra sexual stimulation.

TOP 10 MOVIE SCENES

1. *9 1/2 WEEKS*: MICKEY ROURKE AND KIM BASINGER HAVE SEX ON THE STEPS OF A BUILDING WHILE THE RAIN CASCADES DOWN ON THEM.

2. *THE POSTMAN ALWAYS RINGS TWICE*: JESSICA LANGE AND JACK NICHOLSON MAKE PASSIONATE LOVE ON THE KITCHEN TABLE.

3. *NO WAY OUT*: SEAN YOUNG AND KEVIN COSTNER STEAM UP THE BACK WINDOWS OF A LIMOUSINE.

4. *SLIVER*: SHARON STONE MASTURBATES IN THE BATH.

5. *THE LAST SEDUCTION*: LINDA FIORENTINO HAS A PASSIONATE QUICKIE IN THE ALLEY OUTSIDE A BAR.

6. *THELMA & LOUISE*: BRAD PITT GIVES GEENA DAVIES HER FIRST ORGASM BY ORAL SEX.

7. *SHAKESPEARE IN LOVE*: GWYNETH PALTROW AND JOSEPH FIENNES ENJOY PASSION AND POETRY.

8. *LAST TANGO IN PARIS*: MARLON BRANDO ENJOYS ANAL SEX WITH THE HELP OF SOME BUTTER.

9. *BETTY BLUE*: KNICKERLESS BEATRICE DALLE HAS NONSTOP SEX WITH HER LOVER.

10. *EYES WIDE SHUT*: NICOLE KIDMAN HAS HOT FANTASY SEX WITH A SAILOR.

Historical Sex

BY TAKING SEX OUT OF ITS MODERN
CONTEXT, MANY PEOPLE FEEL THAT
FANTASY ALLOWS THEM TO ENJOY
OUTRAGEOUS SEXUAL ACTS THAT
MIGHT OTHERWISE BE CONSIDERED A
BIT TOO "KINKY," SUCH AS SLAVE
FANTASIES OR VIRGIN SACRIFICES.

All periods of history can be the basis for sexual fantasy, but the rigid rules and cruelty of ancient Rome or Greece, or the master–servant roles in a Victorian-set fantasy are always very popular.

FANTASIES SET IN TIMES THAT HAD STRICT SOCIAL CODES AND BEHAVIOR ARE MOST POPULAR BECAUSE BREAKING THE SEXUAL TABOO IS A PRIME FANTASY TRIGGER.

STORY

A Victorian maid, lowest of the low in a grand Victorian house, is on her hands and knees, scrubbing the floors of the entrance hall. The master of the house enters—handsome and fearsome. He looks at the floor and tells the maid that she is useless and, sitting behind her, roughly grasps her hips, and begins to push her back and forth, like she is scrubbing the floor. Suddenly, he lifts the maid's skirts, undoes his fly, and presses against her. In the middle of the hall floor, defying discovery, the maid suddenly feels the Master enter her.

TOP 10 HISTORICAL SCENES

1. A MAID AND MASTER—ANY PERIOD

2. A VICTORIAN PROSTITUTE AND POLICEMAN

3. A ROMAN SLAVE AND OWNER

4. A 1930S "LADY OF THE MANOR" AND HER HUSBAND'S GAMEKEEPER

5. A COURTESAN AND THE EMPEROR NAPOLEON IN 18TH-CENTURY FRANCE

6. AN AZTEC PRIEST AND A SACRIFICIAL VIRGIN

7. SCARLET O'HARA AND RHET BUTLER IN *GONE WITH THE WIND*

8. NELL GWYNNE AND KING CHARLES AT A ROWDY, HEDONISTIC PALACE BANQUET

9. ACTOR AND ACTRESS IN A 1920S SILENT PORN FILM

10. A SOLDIER GOING OFF TO WAR AND HIS LOVER—CHOOSE ANY CENTURY YOU WISH

Group Sex

A very popular theme, fantasy group sex allows you to explore the notion of being stimulated everywhere at once by several people.

This kind of fantasy can involve anything from one extra person—a friend , stranger, or expartner—to a writhing roomful of bodies. Usually group sex fantasies involve anonymous participants; that is, they exist only as sexual objects rather than real people. This fantasy allows the participants to concentrate on the sex alone.

STORY

Ten attractive men and women, young and old, recline luxuriously in a lush boudoir of soft cushions and erotic drapes, sipping wine from long glasses. The room becomes warm, and the inhabitants begin to remove their clothes. Some start to touch each other, sensually, as the wine takes effect. Lust gradually takes hold of each person in the room, and they begin to stroke each other's genitals; couples and groups caress, and lick and suck the women's breasts. Sex in all sorts of positions begins and the room is filled with the noise of groaning and gasping. Everyone is lost in sensual and sexual pleasure.

Exhibitionism

This fantasy is common among people who long to be admired. It involves either displaying yourself sexually in public, for example, as a lap dancer; or being watched, perhaps through a deliberately left-open window, while naked or having sex. In the fantasy, the onlookers are turned on by your body, your performance, and your sexual power over them.

TOP TEN EXHIBITIONIST SEX FANTASIES

1. BEING TIED UP AND INTIMATELY INSPECTED

2. HAVING SEX ON A POOL TABLE OR A BAR

3. LAP DANCING

4. UNDRESSING IN FRONT OF THE WINDOW AT NIGHT

5. HAVING SEX ON THE DANCE FLOOR OF A NIGHTCLUB

6. BEING A STRIPPER

7. HAVING SEX ON STAGE

8. BEING SPIED ON THROUGH A KEYHOLE

9. BEING PHOTOGRAPHED OR FILMED FOR A PORN VIDEO

10. WEARING TRANSPARENT OR WET CLOTHING IN PUBLIC

Sex Signals

SOMETIMES A FANTASY IS AS BASIC AS HAVING
A MENTAL IMAGE OF AN EROTIC BODY PART,
FOR EXAMPLE, HER BREAST, OR HIS PENIS
THRUSTING IN AND OUT OF HER VAGINA.

This kind of fantasy is more common to men
than women, although both sexes
may focus on a sexual image. This fantasy
picture can often be used to bring on orgasm,
because it doesn't require any thought or
planning. It's simply a sexual trigger that
focuses the mind on what's happening.

STORY

A dancer in a sleazy bar is paid to dance sexily on the tables, to excite the men there. Wearing only a tiny G-string and body oil, she gyrates to slow, thumping music. Although the men can come as close as they like, they're not allowed to touch the dancer, no matter how sensual she chooses to be. The dancer bends over to show her ass and, turning, caresses her breasts and nipples. If she's in the mood, she puts her hand inside her G-string and rubs herself. She removes the G-string and throws it to the audience. Now naked, she starts to masturbate and can see the men rubbing themselves. With a moan, she comes in front of the audience, and leaves the stage.

Discipline

Fantasies involving one person being naughty and being "disciplined" by an authority figure are common, because they appeal to a subversive nature that might seldom be permitted to escape in normal life. Common themes include schoolgirl and teacher, patient and nurse, servant and lord (or lady), or policeman and criminal— any pairing where one of you is in authority. Many people find the idea of transgressing social codes, and crossing a clear sexual boundary, a huge turn-on.

STORY

A naughty schoolgirl (really a fully-developed woman and not a schoolgirl at all) sits down in class. Her legs fall open to show her panties. The teacher calls her to his desk and tells her that she must be punished for being so rude. He takes her to his study and bends her over the desk to spank her. He lifts the girl's skirt and pulls down her panties. But the teacher can't hurt this fragile girl and, instead, caresses her backside and pulls her around onto his lap. The naughty girl knows and enjoys her sexual power. Undoing her blouse, she reveals her breasts and they begin to have sex on the office desk. Another male teacher walks in, but instead of chastising them, joins in.

2 MEN'S **FANTASIES**

MEN AND WOMEN MAY SHARE ELEMENTS OF THEIR SEXUAL FANTASIES, BUT THEY ARE ALSO MARKEDLY DIFFERENT. A WOMAN TENDS TO LOOK AT THE WHOLE PICTURE, WHEREAS MEN NEED MORE OF A SEXUAL "TRIGGER." WOMEN ARE ALSO MENTALLY STIMULATED WHILE MEN ARE MORE VISUALLY AROUSED.

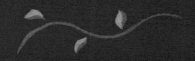

Of course, guys can enjoy elaborate fantasies, but usually only when they're shared —for themselves, they often can't see the point of it. Women may get off on visual stimulation, but will usually construct a hot mental scenario to back it up.

STORY

A man meets up with his ex-girlfriend for a drink in a bar. They drink a bottle of chilled white wine, and both find that their attraction is reignited. They decide to return to his appartment for a night of wild, uninhibited sex where neither has to worry about the niceties of a relationship. The ex-girlfriend undresses herself and frantically undresses him, and kneels on a rug on all fours—she knows what she wants. As the man penetrates her from behind, he watches the reflection of her beautiful breasts swinging in the mirror. Wearing a sexy, triumphant smile on her face, she sighes with pleasure.

ALL A MAN OFTEN NEEDS TO GET GOING IS AN IMAGE—YOU MIGHT SAY THE BRAIN IS LINKED DIRECTLY TO THE PENIS. THE SIMPLER THE IMAGE IS, THE BETTER: CHOOSING A FRIEND OR AN EX-GIRLFRIEND TO FANTASIZE ABOUT IS OFTEN EASIER AND SEXIER THAN INVENTING AN ENCOUNTER WITH A STRANGER.

Men sometimes prefer not to fantasize about unrealistic scenarios: they know Julia Roberts will never be theirs, so why bother dreaming about it? Fantasies about real women are far better. Taking the boss from behind, or finding your sexy neighbor sunbathing naked are more possible to fulfill, and much easier to imagine.

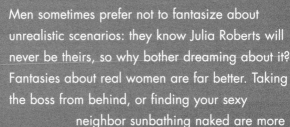

Men can fantasize everywhere
—unlike women, who will often
save a fantasy for long, tedious
bus journeys or moments of
masturbation. Men can fit a
quick fantasy in while
waiting for the kettle
to boil, or changing
their socks.

These fantasies, however, are not brought to fulfillment—they're just a pleasant way to pass time. Many men don't feel the need to fantasize when engaged in actual sex—the sensations are enough for them. For men, most fantasy is an aid to masturbation, especially when pornography, a common tool, is not available.

A GRADUALLY BUILT-UP FANTASY IS IDEAL FOR A LONGER MASTURBATION SESSION. MEN MAY ACTUALLY THINK THROUGH AN ENTIRE SCENARIO, RATHER THAN HAVING A FIVE MINUTE "LOOKING AT BREASTS" FANTASY, WHICH CAN BE USED WHEN TIME IS SHORT.

If guys are fantasizing during sex, it's likely to be simple; for example, that he's with a beautiful supermodel, or that she's giving him the best blow-job of his entire life. Because men are visually more easy to stimulate than women, he won't need anything too complicated.

CASE STUDY

"I FANTASIZE WHEN I'M ON MY OWN IN THE HOUSE—USUALLY IT'LL LEAD TO MASTURBATION, AND I DON'T ALWAYS WANT MY GIRLFRIEND TO KNOW WHAT I'M DOING. THERE'S SOMETHING QUITE SEXY ABOUT AN EMPTY HOUSE—I LIKE TO WALK AROUND NAKED OR WITH JUST A BATHROBE ON, AND I FIND IT VERY SENSUAL AND EXCITING TO BE NAKED SOMEWHERE YOU SHOULD BE CLOTHED, LIKE IN THE KITCHEN. SOMETIMES I'LL MASTURBATE IN THE SHOWER LIKE IN THE SCENE FROM *AMERICAN BEAUTY*. IT HIDES ANY NOISE I MAKE WHEN I COME."

Paul, 28, Town Planner

CASE STUDY

"I LOVE TO TELL MY PARTNER STORIES—THEY TURN US BOTH ON. SHE GETS EMBARRASSED, SO I MAKE THEM UP AND WHISPER THEM TO HER AS WE'RE MAKING LOVE. I TELL HER ONE ABOUT A PRISON WARDER WHO'S GUARDING A WOMAN PRISONER, AND SEDUCES HER IN THE CELL. I GO INTO A LOT OF DETAIL, ABOUT THE SOUNDS AND HOW IT LOOKS, AND WHAT HAPPENS. THE STORIES REALLY EXCITE ME—I DRAW ON FILMS I'VE SEEN OR BOOKS I'VE READ. I TRY TO MATCH WHAT I'M SAYING TO WHAT I'M DOING TO MY GIRLFRIEND. WE BOTH HAVE OUR BEST ORGASMS AFTER ONE OF THESE SESSIONS."

Jonathan, 28, Builder

Masturbation

PORNOGRAPHY OFFERS AN EASY ROUTE FOR
MASTURBATORY FANTASY, BECAUSE PICTURES
PROVIDE AN INSTANT TURN-ON WITHOUT THE
DISTRACTIONS OF EMOTION, SCENARIOS, OR
WORDS. HOWEVER, IF YOUR PARTNER REALLY
OBJECTS TO PORN, YOU CAN BE EQUALLY
TURNED ON BY POLAROIDS OF YOUR PARTNER
IN PORNOGRAPHIC POSES.

CASE STUDY

"I ALWAYS NEED PORN TO MASTURBATE. I CAN'T
CONCENTRATE ON MENTAL IMAGES, BECAUSE I'VE
ALWAYS USED A MAGAZINE—NOTHING TOO
HARDCORE, JUST NAKED GIRLS. THEY TURN ME
ON: THEY'RE BEAUTIFUL TO LOOK AT AND THAT'S
WHAT THE MAGAZINES ARE THERE FOR. I TRIED
INTERNET PORN, BUT IT DIDN'T FEEL REAL.
MAGAZINES ARE SLIGHTLY MORE RAUNCHY. MY
GIRLFRIEND KNOWS AND SAYS SHE DOESN'T
MIND, AS LONG AS I PREFER HER IN REAL LIFE—
WHICH OF COURSE I DO; THE GIRLS IN THE MAGS
ARE JUST A TRIGGER TO HELP ME MASTURBATE."

Graham, 29, Account Executive

Men often take their sexual triggers from their early experiences with pornography. Porn models in reality tend to be girl-next-door types: no man wants to be threatened in his own fantasy, so the characters in male fantasies will often be approachable and pretty, without being too glamorous and outrageous.

Threesome

Fantasizing about a threesome (two girls and a guy) is a simple desire for more sexual attention. Almost all men dream of having two girls playing with them, licking them, or penetrating one while the other stimulates them. It involves less emotion than one-to-one sex, and is simply about the sheer enjoyment of doubling your sexual pleasure and the sensation of being touched all over at once.

The threesome is a fantasy that you can enact in real life—but be careful. You're involving another's emotions, and a guy might feel more jealous than he'd anticipated if his girl enjoyed the other woman more. On the other hand, the girl might enjoy it far less than she'd thought, and this would cause embarrassment all around. Make sure that you're all completely happy with what's happening before you begin.

CASE STUDY

"I WAS ALWAYS OBSESSED WITH THE IDEA OF A THREESOME—IT WAS MY FAVORITE FANTASY FOR YEARS. LATER, A GIRL I WENT OUT WITH WAS VERY SEXUALLY UNINHIBITED AND SHE SAID SHE'D TRY IT IF I WANTED. WE INVITED A BISEXUAL FRIEND AROUND, WE ALL GOT DRUNK AND MY GIRLFRIEND MADE A PASS AT HER. INITIALLY IT WAS A HUGE TURN-ON FOR ME TO WATCH THEM, BUT THEY SEEMED TO BE SO INVOLVED WITH EACH OTHER THERE WAS NO ROOM FOR ME. I FELT LIKE A SORDID VOYEUR, AND A BIT JEALOUS. SHE LOVED IT AND WANTED TO DO IT AGAIN, BUT MY FAVORITE FANTASY WAS RUINED."

Barry, 32, Musician

CASE STUDY

"MY GIRLFRIEND HAD EXPERIENCED THREESOMES BEFORE WE MET, AND SAID SHE'D DO IT WITH A MAN BUT NOT WITH A WOMAN. WE ESTABLISHED THAT SHE WOULDN'T HAVE SEX WITH HIM (I'M PRETTY SECURE BUT I COULDN'T HANDLE SEEING SOMEONE ELSE HAVE SEX WITH HER) AND WE ASKED AN EX OF HERS, WHOM SHE'S STILL FRIENDLY WITH. HE AND I DIDN'T REALLY TOUCH, BUT WATCHING HIM TOUCH HER REALLY TURNED ME ON. IT ENDED WHEN HE WENT DOWN ON HER AND THEN SHE AND I HAD SEX WHILE SHE GAVE HIM A HAND-JOB. IT WAS AN INCREDIBLE NIGHT FOR ALL THREE OF US."

Alan, 26, Teacher

Bondage

Many men love to feel powerless, both physically and sexually. Being tied up removes all expectation, and leaves them vulnerable and unable to fight—a sensation that's very liberating for a lot of men who are used to having a protective, dominating role. Letting a woman take charge of them is sexy because they are entirely at the mercy of their partner.

BONDAGE FANTASIES CAN WORK IN REALITY IN SOME WAYS. IF YOU WANT TO BE HANGING FROM THE CEILING IN A CAVE, YOU CAN VERY EASILY SET THE SCENE AND MAKE UP STORIES WHILE YOU TIE YOUR LOVER TO THE BED.

Find out what aspect of this fantasy appeals to your man, and construct a fantasy accordingly using stories and dialog. Domination is a good starting point; for example, you might begin with: "Now I'm going to tie you up, because your behavior's been so bad."

STORY

A young, blonde headmistress enters a classroom. Her hair is pulled back in a bun and she's wearing a tight, black suit that hugs her thighs and breasts. A man sits at a desk, dressed as a schoolboy in shorts. She's come to talk to him about his bad behavior. The boy is told that he is going to be punished and, removing a small whip from her bag, she slaps him across the legs. The boy cries out in pain and she smiles. The headmistress undoes the boy's fly and pulls his pants down, telling him that he mustn't touch himself because he's been naughty. She alternates between whipping and fondling the boy, until he's begging her to do more. Finally, the mistress is overcome with lust, raising her skirt and unbuttoning her blouse.

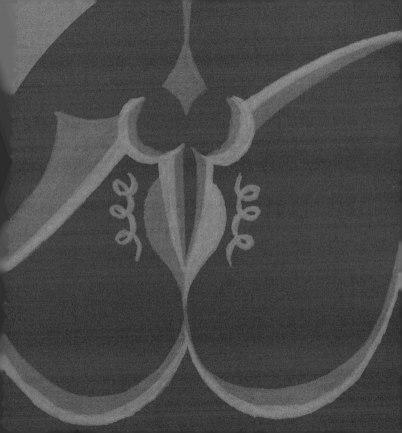

CASE STUDY

"I IMAGINE A GIRL—MY BEAUTIFUL GIRLFRIEND OR
EX-GIRLFRIEND—ENTERING MY BEDROOM, WHERE I'M
NAKED. SHE WANTS ME, AND TAKES A LENGTH OF
ROPE AND TIES MY ARMS ABOVE MY HEAD AND
LASHES MY ANKLES TO THE BOTTOM OF THE BED.
WHAT SHE DOES AFTER THAT VARIES—SOMETIMES
IT'S A BLOW-JOB THAT DRIVES ME MAD WITH
EXCITEMENT BECAUSE I CAN'T MOVE, OR, SHE
CLIMBS ON TOP OF ME AND HAS SEX. I LOVE THE
FANTASY BECAUSE IT'S SO EROTIC, YET I DON'T HAVE
TO DO ANYTHING—THE POWER'S ALL HERS."

Thomas, 35, Doctor

Watching Two Women

The lesbian fantasy is an old favorite. Men argue that two naked women getting it on together doubles a man's pleasure; that seeing women arouse each other sexually is a great turn-on. In the fantasy, however, the women always want him to join in. He begins by watching them and, perhaps, masturbating, but by the end of the fantasy he is involved too.

STORY

A man returns to his partner's appartment early from a night on the town. Much to his surprise, he finds his girlfriend and a very attractive female friend of hers kissing passionately. Though shocked, he is aroused as he watches the girls undress and continue to touch each other. The man's girlfriend turns to face him, and beckons him over. The girls undress him and both go down on him, sucking and licking and stroking him while he touches their genitals with his hands. The excitment lasts for hours as they change positions and caress each other with their bodies. The man has sex with both women and they all finally collapse, exhausted.

Orgies

A SEXUAL FREE-FOR-ALL IS A VERY COMMON MALE
FANTASY BECAUSE IT ALLOWS HIM TO ENVISAGE
COMMITMENT-FREE SEX, WITH NOBODY ASKING
"BUT DO YOU REALLY LOVE ME?" AFTERWARD. IN
OTHER WORDS, A MAN CAN INDULGE HIMSELF
WITH ONLY THE PHYSICAL ASPECT. THE FANTASY
OFTEN INVOLVES WOMEN ONLY—THE IDEA OF
BREASTS EVERYWHERE YOU LOOK CAN BE THRILLING.

In some orgy fantasies, there might be as much enjoyment
in simply watching as there is in joining in. Or, you might
find there is even a bit of both…

STORY

A Roman theme party has been organized by a local group, and many of the women are wearing barely-there togas. The wine is flowing and everyone is enjoying themselves. As the evening wears on, some of the party-goers begin to caress one another in a drunkenly uninhibited way. They feed each other grapes and, removing their clothes, pour red wine all over others' bodies, and lick it off. In a halcyon haze, everyone is suddenly having sex in every kind of position, with tangles of naked men and women of all ages, gasping and groaning ecstatically.

Uninhibited Sex

THE MAJORITY OF MEN WISH THEIR PARTNERS
WOULD ACCEPT THAT THEY FIND THEM DESPERATELY
ATTRACTIVE, BECAUSE, THEY SAY, A CONFIDENT
WOMAN TENDS TO BE LESS INHIBITED IN BED. IT IS
ALSO A REASON WHY MEN OFTEN FANTASIZE
ABOUT SEX WITH NO BARRIERS—PURE,
UNADULTERATED SEX IN EVERY POSITION, WITH A
PARTNER WHO IS WEARING THE SEXIEST
UNDERWEAR EVER. VERY SIMPLE, YET VERY EFFECTIVE.

Gain the trust of your lover by understanding her needs and emotions, by making her feel special, important, and essentially, great in bed. Through this she will feel more confident and willing to try out new ideas.

CASE STUDY

"MY WIFE IS BEAUTIFUL BUT VERY SHY: SHE DOESN'T LIKE TO GET UNDRESSED IN FRONT OF ME, AND SHE LIKES THE LIGHTS OFF DURING SEX. SHE'S A LOVING PARTNER, BUT DOESN'T FIND IT EASY TO LET GO. MY FANTASY IS THAT ONE DAY SHE'LL TAKE THE INITIATIVE WHEREVER WE HAPPEN TO BE (IN MY IMAGINATION, IT'S SOMETIMES THE CAR, OR A WOOD). SHE TAKES OUT MY PENIS AND IS REALLY EXCITED BY IT—SHE GOES DOWN ON ME, ENJOYING IT, AND THEN CLIMBS ON TOP, NAKED, AND SCREWS ME TILL SHE HAS A MASSIVE ORGASM. SHE ISN'T LIKE THIS AT ALL IN REAL LIFE, BUT I ALWAYS HOPE THAT ONE DAY…"

Andy, 28, Development Officer

TOP TEN MALE FANTASIES

1. UNENDING AND NUMEROUS BLOW-JOBS

2. WATCHING TWO WOMEN MAKE LOVE AND JOINING IN

3. WATCHING A WOMAN UNDRESS AND MASTURBATE

4. BEING TIED UP AND FORCED INTO SUBMISSION

5. BEING DISCIPLINED BY A SEXY WOMAN

6. MAKING LOVE WITH A BEAUTIFUL OR FAMOUS WOMAN

7. HAVING SEX OUTSIDE OR IN PUBLIC

8. BEING DESIRED BY SEVERAL SEXY WOMEN, AND HAVING ALL OF THEM

9. HAVING A VERY PREDATORY WOMAN TEACH YOU SEX TECHNIQUES

10. HAVING A SUBMISSIVE WOMAN, OR VIRGIN, GIVING IN TO YOUR SEDUCTION

Oral Sex

MEN LOVE ORAL SEX: SOMETIMES GIVING IT, BUT ALMOST ALWAYS RECEIVING IT. UNLESS THEY ARE VERY INHIBITED, IT'S LIKELY THAT A BLOW-JOB IS ONE OF THEIR MOST COMMON FANTASIES. GIVEN THAT MOST YOUNG MEN APPARENTLY THINK ABOUT SEX EVERY 15 MINUTES, THIS ADDS UP TO QUITE A FEW FANTASY BLOW-JOBS.

STORY

A young couple sit in the back of a car one night while their friend drives it down the freeway. The girl, who is very attractive, begins to slide down the seat until her head is in her partner's lap. She slowly, lovingly, unzips the boy's fly and gently pulls out his penis, and, putting her mouth around it, starts to suck slowly. She steadily sucks, licks, and flicks with her tongue, being careful of any sudden jerky movements. The boy is almost blind with ecstasy, desire, and frustration; moans of pleasure threaten to emerge from his mouth but, because of the driver's presence, he must stay silent throughout this, his exquisite torture.

Anal Sex

Anal sex is still considered unusual, so many men love the idea for its naughtiness. This transgression of normal codes also has a hint of homosexuality, a feeling that arouses some men. On the whole it remains a fantasy because in reality, it can be difficult to do, and many people, both men and women, are afraid that it's unhygienic.

CASE STUDY

"I HAVE NEVER HAD ANAL SEX, BUT IN MY IMAGINATION MY PARTNER OFFERS IT TO ME AND I CAN'T WAIT TO TRY IT. I LUBRICATE MY PENIS AND PUSH IT BY SLOW DEGREES INSIDE HER. IT FEELS INCREDIBLY TIGHT—MORE LIKE BEING HELD BY A FIST THAN A VAGINA. IT'S VERY EXCITING BECAUSE IT FEELS TABOO: IT'S THE ONE PLACE YOU'RE NOT ALLOWED TO GO BECAUSE IT'S TOTALLY PRIVATE. IN MY FANTASY, MY PARTNER LOVES WHAT I'M DOING AND I REACH AROUND TO PLAY WITH HER VAGINA AND CLITORIS AS WELL. MY PARTNER WOULD NEVER LET ME DO THIS IN REALITY."

Patrick, 34, IT Consultant

Water Sports

SOME MEN ARE EXCITED BY THE NOTION
OF PEEING ON THEIR PARTNERS, OR
HAVING IT DONE TO THEM. IN REALITY
THEY MAY BE DISGUSTED BY THE IDEA,
BUT SOME MEN LOVE THE FANTASY—A
TABOO SUBJECT ALWAYS HAS THE
POTENTIAL TO BE HIGHLY EROTIC.

Allowing yourself to be peed on is a highly
submissive state to be in, and using the penis as a
spray-gun on someone else is very dominating. It's very
"dirty" sex (in every sense), and an arousing fantasy.

CASE STUDY

"I WOULD NEVER DO THIS IN REAL LIFE, BUT THE IDEA OF BEING PEED ON BY A SEXY GIRL HAS ALWAYS TURNED ME ON. IN MY FANTASY, A STRANGE WOMAN, PERHAPS A HOOKER, COMES OVER TO WHERE I'M LYING, SAYS SHE'S DESPERATE FOR A PEE, AND ASKS WHETHER I MIND IF SHE GOES AHEAD. I TELL HER TO FEEL FREE. SHE SQUATS OVER ME AND LETS IT GO ALL OVER MY GENITALS. IT FEELS WARM AND AROUSING; I DON'T FEEL UNCLEAN AT ALL. THE IDEA THAT SHE COULD LET GO TO THAT EXTENT REALLY TURNS ME ON."

Ritchie, 40, Photographer

Virgins

Many men share a desire to be the first to have sex with a virgin and, as a fantasy, it's incredibly popular. Of course, the fantasy virgin is rarely inept or unsure of how to roll on a condom. They are more likely to be a glamorous Pamela Anderson-type figure with a bad case of amnesia, who says: "I know I'm going to love this, but would you mind showing me what to do?"

VIRGINS ARE, IN MANY MEN'S EYES, THE ULTIMATE "SEXUAL TROPHY." IF A WOMAN IS PREPARED TO GIVE A MAN HER MOST PRECIOUS ASSET, HE MUST BE ONE HELL OF A GUY.

As a role-play, this one is easy—all your partner needs is a virginal white nightdress, an air of innocence, and off you go.

STORY

There's a girl of about seventeen, very attractive and curvy, who has a naughty twinkle in her eyes. A handsome man starts chatting with her, and asks if she's a virgin. The girl says that she is, although she doesn't want to be for much longer. She asks, hopefully, if the man can help her lose her virginity. Agreeing, he undresses her. Her body is young, firm, and lovely, and he is thrilled, knowing that nobody else has seen it and he is the first. The man is full of lust but penetrates her carefully, and she cries out with shock and excitement at her newfound sexual thrill.

3 WOMEN'S **FANTASIES**

WOMEN'S FANTASIES TEND TO BE MUCH MORE COMPLEX THAN MEN'S; A WOMAN GENERALLY NEEDS MORE THAN A PORNOGRAPHIC IMAGE TO GET HER GOING SEXUALLY.

EITHER A STRONG, DETAILED MEMORY OF A SEXUAL ENCOUNTER, AN EROTIC STORY, OR A THOROUGHLY FLESHED-OUT SEXUAL FANTASY AS COMPLEX AS ANY FEATURE FILM, WITH HERSELF STARRING, IS WHAT WILL GET ANY WOMAN SEXUALLY EXCITED.

Women enjoy focusing on details—how they're being touched, where they imagine they are, and who with. If their imagination isn't working, they'll probably be far less turned on by the actual sex in the fantasy. The broader picture doesn't always work for a woman, and sometimes she'll need to imagine the environment in detail and exactly what her dream lover looks like and says, in order to believe in it enough to become fully aroused.

CASE STUDY

"I IMAGINE I'M A HOOKER WHO WORKS IN A HIGH-CLASS MASSAGE PARLOR. JUST THE IDEA OF IT ISN'T ENOUGH FOR ME THOUGH—I HAVE TO IMAGINE THE WHOLE THING, FROM WHAT THE ROOM LOOKS LIKE TO THE FACES OF THE CUSTOMERS. IT'S VERY OPULENT AND THE MEN ARE ALL RICH, OLDER EUROPEAN TYPES AND QUITE SEXY. I EVEN IMAGINE THE CONVERSATIONS I HAVE WITH THEM BEFORE I START TURNING THEM ON. IT HELPS ME TO FOCUS COMPLETELY ON MY SENSATIONS WHEN I'M TOUCHING MYSELF—I GET SO CAUGHT UP IN THE FANTASY THAT REAL LIFE DOESN'T INTRUDE AT ALL."

Simone, 29, Nurse

THERE'S LESS DISTINCTION BETWEEN WOMEN'S MASTURBATORY FANTASIES AND THEIR SEXUAL FANTASIES THAN THERE IS FOR MEN. DURING MASTURBATION, A WOMAN CAN ENVISAGE ANY SCENARIO, BECAUSE HER ABILITY TO IMPROVISE SEXUAL SCENES IS MUCH GREATER THAN A MAN'S. AND IF SHE FINDS FOUR OR FIVE IDEAS THAT WORK, SHE'LL RETURN TO THEM DURING SEX, ADDING REFINEMENTS EACH TIME. SOME WOMEN CAN RETAIN THE SAME BASIC FANTASY FROM EARLY ADOLESCENCE TO ADULTHOOD AND CUSTOMIZE IT EVERY TIME.

YOU MAY FANTASIZE ABOUT REAL MEN
OR WOMEN YOU KNOW BUT YOU ARE MORE
LIKELY TO FOCUS ON YOUR OWN ROLE,
IMAGINING YOURSELF AS THE MAIN
CHARACTER. OFTEN THE PARTNER'S ROLE IS
ALMOST INCIDENTAL.

CASE STUDY

"When I'm masturbating I have about five favorite fantasies and, like using a mental filing box, I find the one that fits my mood, and adjust it slightly. Then I just lie back and go with it. They're quite detailed. One fantasy is about being a plane passenger who's called into the cockpit to meet the crew. I admire the instruments, then the pilot leans over and runs his hand up my leg—and we end up with him going down on me as we cruise along. My fantasies really help me to feel horny, and definitely make me come faster."

Angela, 25, Manager

FANTASIES THAT YOU USE WHEN DAYDREAMING OR MASTURBATING CAN, OF COURSE, INCLUDE YOUR PARTNER—AND BECAUSE THEY ARE FANTASIES, YOU CAN IMAGINE THEY'RE ENJOYING THINGS YOU KNOW THEY MIGHT NEVER AGREE TO IN REALITY.

Women don't necessarily involve emotion in their fantasies—they too can have completely unadulterated fantasy sex, where they are under no pressure to behave in an acceptable way.

CASE STUDY

"I'VE FANTASIZED ABOUT CELEBRITIES SINCE I
WAS ABOUT 12; IMAGINING SOMEONE SO
POWERFUL WANTING ME IS AN APHRODISIAC.
THE FANTASIES USUALLY START WITH ME BEING
INVITED ONTO A FILM SET. THE MALE STAR
KEEPS GLANCING OVER AT ME, THEN HE
BECKONS ME OVER TO HIS TRAILER. INSIDE, HE
PUSHES UP MY SKIRT WITHOUT A WORD AND
PULLS ME ONTO HIS KNEE AND WE HAVE FAST,
FRANTIC SEX. THE CREW OUTSIDE ARE UNAWARE.
IF I EVER MET MY FANTASY CELEBRITIES IN REAL
LIFE, I WOULDN'T HAVE A WORD TO SAY."

Diane, 32, Shop Worker

Remember, women are capable of enjoying those kind of fantasies that, if anyone offered in reality, would have them running a mile. Forced sex, bondage, pain, coercion, and humiliation might have a part—but this doesn't mean they really want to experience any of them.

The Stranger

A favorite fantasy involves a stranger who simply desires your body, and for whom you don't have to remember his mother's birthday or pick up his dry cleaning. You can present yourself in your imagination as the wildest thing—even if in real life you're a lights-out girl. You can be entirely uninhibited.

OFTEN, THE FANTASY STRANGER WILL APPEAR
WITHIN A RECOGNIZABLE CONTEXT, FOR EXAMPLE,
THE PLUMBER, THE BUILDER, OR THE MAN WHO
WALKS PAST YOU IN THE STREET EVERY
MORNING. ALTERNATIVELY, IT MIGHT
BE A RANDOM CUSTOMER IN
A NIGHTCLUB WHO ONLY
EXISTS IN YOUR HEAD.

Sex with a stranger can be enacted in real life, but you really have to be careful and know exactly what you're doing. You might pick someone up in a bar and have sex with him in the men's restroom, but be aware of the health risks involved, and that the reality might not be quite as exciting as your fantasy. Furthermore, he might not be the normal guy that he seems.

STORY

A woman is lounging around her house, wearing just a towel, when the doorbell rings. It's a man who wants her to fill in a survey. She invites him in, noticing how attractive he is. She lets the towel slip very slightly so he can see the tops of her breasts. As she bends to get a pen, she knows she's really turning him on and she "accidentally" lets the towel slip to the floor. Suddenly he's behind her, with his hands on her breasts, teasing her nipples. They immediately have urgent, hot sex on top of the kitchen table.

CASE STUDY

"I HAVE HAD SEX WITH A STRANGER. I MET HIM AT A ROCK FESTIVAL; WE KEPT EXCHANGING GLANCES WHILE THE BAND WERE PLAYING. HE BECKONED ME OVER, AND I WENT. WE NECKED FOR A WHILE, THEN HE TOOK MY HAND AND LED ME TO HIS TENT NEARBY, WHERE WE HAD FAST, FRANTIC SEX, PRACTICALLY WITHOUT SPEAKING. I ONLY FOUND OUT HIS NAME AFTERWARD. I HAD A CIGARETTE AND LEFT, BUT I NEVER FELT BAD ABOUT IT—THE WHOLE EXPERIENCE WAS FANTASTIC. REMEMBERING THAT DAY IS ONE OF MY FAVORITE FANTASIES."

Adeline, 30, Dancer

"Forced" Sex

"Forced" sex in the imagination is naturally a very different scenario from real-life rape. In this type of fantasy many women imagine that they are having sex against their will, but they get more and more excited until it is very much what they want. Because this fantasy is only in the woman's mind the woman is, of course, totally in control.

"FORCED" SEX FANTASIES CAN INVOLVE SOME PHYSICAL RESTRAINT SO THAT YOU CAN'T STRUGGLE AGAINST YOUR LOVER —OR THEY SIMPLY INVOLVE BEING FORCIBLY HELD DOWN AND "TAKEN." SOME FEEL THAT IT IS EROTIC NOT TO BE IN CONTROL. OTHERS MIGHT LIKE THE IDEA THAT THEY'RE ENJOYING THEM-SELVES WHEN THEY'RE NOT SUPPOSED TO BE. WITH BONDAGE, IT CAN BE JUST THE THOUGHT OF WHAT MIGHT HAPPEN, RATHER THAN WHAT DOES (EVEN IN FANTASIES), THAT IS THE BIG TURN-ON.

CASE STUDY

"IT'S HARD TO CONFESS THAT I GET TURNED ON BY IMAGINING MYSELF BEING FORCED INTO SEX, BUT IT'S TRUE. I DEVELOPED A FANTASY THAT MY BOYFRIEND WAS A BURGLAR WHO HAD BROKEN IN, AND I HAD TO HAVE SEX WITH HIM SO HE WOULDN'T KILL ME. IN THE FANTASY, HE SAID FILTHY THINGS TO ME, AND CALLED ME A SLUT AND A WHORE—JUST THINKING ABOUT IT TURNED ME ON. OF COURSE IN REALITY IT WOULD BE HELLISH BUT, IN MY MIND, IT FREED ME TO ENJOY THE SENSATIONS I WAS FEELING WITHOUT ANY GUILT."

Caroline, 29, Designer

STORY

One night a woman sees a big, macho guy looking at her in a hotel bar. Glancing again in her direction, the man gets up and walks out. The woman, curious, follows him to a bedroom, where the man closes the door behind them. It's clear he wants her badly, and he immediately throws her up against the wall of the room. The woman feebly murmurs "No, no," but in truth she's incredibly turned on—she really wants him inside her. He pins her arms above her head and thrusts into her, with no foreplay, and they immediately have frenzied, desperate sex.

The Threesome

TWO SUN-TANNED, FIT, AND HANDSOME MEN
SWARM ALL OVER YOUR BODY—YOU MAY FLESH
OUT THE DETAILS A LITTLE MORE THAN THIS, BUT
THE RESULT IS USUALLY THE SAME.

The idea of two men desiring you at once, two pairs of
hands and two tongues looking after your every need, will
make your orgasm hugely intensified. You might be with
your real-life lover or you might not—it's up to you.

BE CAREFUL IF YOU WANT TO TRY A THREESOME IN REAL LIFE—SEX WITH TWO MEN CAN BE HARD WORK. MEN CAN ALSO BECOME VERY JEALOUS AND WANT ALL THE ATTENTION, OR, THE TWO GUYS MIGHT REALLY BE GETTING IT ON, AND YOU'LL BE LEFT WONDERING WHY YOU'RE THERE. WOMEN DO HAVE EMOTIONS, AND IT MIGHT BE HARD TO SHARE THEM OUT. ONLY TRY IT IF YOU'RE VERY SURE THAT EVERYONE IS WILLING AND SENSIBLE ABOUT WHAT THEY ARE GOING TO DO.

STORY

Two men are taking turns to go down on a woman. They're both really turned on, and are vying for her attention. She takes a penis in each hand, and gives them both hand-jobs while they stimulate her to orgasm. Eventually the woman has sex with them both at the same time, with one in her vagina and one in her anus, gasping with pleasure. Knowing that she can take two men at once, and that they both want her, makes her feel like the hottest thing.

SEX WITH TWO WOMEN AND
A MAN? YOU MIGHT FIND
YOURSELF IN YOUR PARTNER'S
FANTASY RATHER THAN YOUR
OWN. AGAIN, IF EVERYONE TAKES
EQUAL PLEASURE AND AN EQUAL
SHARE, THEN IT CAN WORK.

Sex With A Woman

Fantasies of lesbian sex are attractive to many women. Some consider lesbian sex "forbidden," which therefore makes it more arousing. Knowing that another woman is feeling the same as you when you turn her on is very erotic. There may or may not be penetration, depending on whether your fantasy lesbian is submissive or dominant—you might find yourself with a lesbian who wears a strap-on.

STORY

A woman lies on a bed, with a strange woman touching her. The stranger really turns the woman on, touching and caressing her breasts and between her legs. She stops asks the woman to do the same to her. Nervous at first, the woman soon understands what the stranger wants. The stranger begins to get really hot, then gives her a strap-on penis. The woman turns her over onto all fours, and penetrates her, enjoying the unusual sensation of power as the stranger pants and moans.

A woman might imagine herself as someone who is desired for her sexuality, such as a stripper, a lap dancer, or a prostitute. You may enjoy the thought that you can turn men on without necessarily touching them—the woman is in control of the men's excitement.

Women can also be turned on by the type of reaction they produce in a man; for example, in noticing the bulge in a man's pants, or seeing a man in the shower through a window and the man becoming unexpectedly hard.

BOTH MEN AND WOMEN FANTASIZE ABOUT BEING WATCHED WHILE THEY HAVE SEX—EITHER BY A SINGLE PERSON OR BY A GROUP. THE ONLOOKERS MIGHT BE ANYONE FROM A PASSERBY (WATCHING A COUPLE HAVE SEX IN A CAR) TO A COLONY OF ALIENS (WHERE THE WOMAN HAS BEEN "TAKEN" FOR SEXUAL "EXPERIMENTATION"). THIS TYPE OF FANTASY CAN BE ENJOYED IN THE BEDROOM BY BOTH PARTNERS, THROUGH STORYTELLING.

WOMEN CAN FIND THE
FANTASY OF BEING LOOKED
AT BY A STRANGER AS
THEY LIE OR STAND NAKED
(ON A BED, BY AN OPEN
WINDOW, OR IN THE
SHOWER) A REAL TURN-ON.

FANTASIES OF WATCHING A MAN
MASTURBATE ARE VERY COMMON,
WHETHER YOU IMAGINE YOUR
BOYFRIEND MASTURBATING OVER YOU,
OR A MAN MASTURBATING AND
WATCHING THROUGH YOUR
WINDOW AS YOU UNDRESS.

CASE STUDY

"I ALWAYS MASTURBATE IN FRONT OF A MIRROR. SEEING MY BODY RESPOND TO MY OWN TOUCH IS VERY EXCITING FOR ME, AND OCCASIONALLY, I WILL MOVE THE MIRROR SO I CAN'T SEE MY FACE. THEN I FEEL LIKE AN ANONYMOUS PORN ACTRESS, TURNING EVERYONE ON BY RUBBING MYSELF HARD, OR TWEAKING MY NIPPLES TO MAKE THEM STAND OUT. SOMETIMES I MASSAGE BODY OIL INTO MY SKIN AND ADMIRE IT GLISTENING. I LIKE MY BODY AND I LOOK AT IT AS A MAN WOULD—AS A VERY SEXY, DESIRABLE VISION!"

Alison, 28, Public Relations Executive

THE "BEING-WATCHED" FANTASY IS EASY AND FUN TO TRY OUT IN EVERYDAY SEX. FOR EXAMPLE, AS A FANTASY LAP-DANCER YOU CAN DRESS UP IN SEXY BLACK LACE LINGERIE, SHINY, PVC STOCKINGS, AND HIGH HEELS—WHATEVER YOUR SCENARIO SUGGESTS. DANCE AND STRIP TO SOME MUSIC WHILE YOUR "PAYING CUSTOMER" WATCHES— AND REMEMBER TO CHARGE HIM.

Having your lover tuck money into your stocking or G-string makes a stripper or lap-dancer game authentic, and shows that he's really enjoying the show and wants more.

CASE STUDY

"I IMAGINE I'M WEARING A LITTLE BLACK G-STRING AND MAYBE NIPPLE TASSELS, AND THAT I'M DANCING FOR CLIENTS. THERE'S ONE CUSTOMER IN PARTICULAR WHO'S SHY, AND IT'S MY JOB TO DRAW HIM OUT AND GIVE HIM A GOOD TIME. I PERFORM A REALLY DIRTY DANCE ROUTINE FOR HIM. HE'S OVERCOME WITH LUST AND REACHES FORWARD TO LICK MY BREASTS. AT THIS POINT, I FORGET WHERE I AM AND GIVE IN TO MY URGES. WE HAVE SEX RIGHT THERE, IN FRONT OF EVERYONE."

Jeanette, 29, Mature Student

CASE STUDY

"I AM A BIT OF AN EXHIBITIONIST—
I SOMETIMES GET UNDRESSED WITH
THE CURTAINS OPEN, AND OFTEN
HAVE SEX OUTDOORS. ALL MY FANTASIES
INVOLVE BEING WATCHED AND DESIRED. I
IMAGINE MEN GETTING TURNED ON BY ME
WHEN I'M NAKED, POLE-DANCING, OR STRIPPING
FOR THEM. SOMETIMES I IMAGINE I'M IN A SEEDY
BAR ON A POOL TABLE BEING PENETRATED AND
THERE'S A BIG CROWD OF MEN ALL WATCHING AND
WAITING FOR THEIR TURN WITH ME. IT SOUNDS
DEGRADING, BUT IN MY MIND IT'S VERY SEXY."

Rhiannon, 30, Office Worker

TOP TEN FEMALE FANTASIES

1. BEING CAUGHT BY AUTHORITY FIGURE DURING SEX

2. GOING OUT IN TRANSPARENT CLOTHES OR WITH NO UNDERWEAR ON

3. A ROMANCE, SUCH AS MAKING LOVE IN A FOUR POSTER BED, OR BEING SWEPT AWAY BY A PASSIONATE RHET BUTLER FROM *GONE WITH THE WIND*

4. SEX WITH A COLLEAGUE AT WORK

5. BEING MADE LOVE TO BY TWO OR MORE MEN AT THE SAME TIME

6. SEX WITH A CELEBRITY

7. SEX ON THE BEACH

8. BEING A DEFLOWERED OR SACRIFICIAL VIRGIN

9. HAVING BEAUTIFUL YOUNG MEN AS SEX SLAVES

10. SEDUCING A MAN WHO IS JUST A FRIEND

Having An Affair

A fantasy as simple as sex with someone other than their regular partner is common to many women. The allure of the guy at work, the stranger on the bus, or the man next door, can plunge her into a fevered daydream about their passionate lovemaking.

THE FANTASY AFFAIR IS A GOOD WAY OF ENJOYING SEXUAL EXPERIENCES THAT YOU COULDN'T IMAGINE WORKING WITH YOUR PARTNER. FOR EXAMPLE, YOU MIGHT IMAGINE HAVING SEX WITH YOUR BOSS ON HIS DESK, WHEREAS YOUR PARTNER WOULD BE HORRIFIED BY THE IDEA OF HIM HAVING SEX IN THE SAME SCENARIO. A MORE EXTREME EXAMPLE WOULD BE HAVING ELABORATE BONDAGE FANTASIES INVOLVING YOUR DENTIST.

CASE STUDY

"MY FAVORITE FANTASY IS ABOUT A GUY I WORK WITH. NOTHING WILL EVER HAPPEN, BUT IN MY FANTASY I IMAGINE WE'RE WORKING ON A PROJECT TOGETHER LATE AT NIGHT. WE'RE THE ONLY PEOPLE LEFT IN THE OFFICE AND I ASK HIM IF HE WANTS A COFFEE. HE SAYS, 'I JUST WANT YOU,' AND PUSHES ME DOWN ONTO THE DESK, LIFTING MY SKIRT UP. HE ENTERS ME AND WE HAVE PASSIONATE, HARD SEX. I OCCASIONALLY ALLOW MYSELF THIS FANTASY AT WORK AND IT MAKES ME SMILE TO SEE HIM AND KNOW HE HASN'T GOT A CLUE."

Bella, 28, Designer

Sacrifice

The fantasy of being "sacrificed" to some ancient god, or handed over as payment in a deal, is a recurring one in the fantasies of many women. It's a combination of being treated entirely as a sex object—chosen for being the prettiest or the sexiest—in a way that might never happen (and you may not want it to) in real life.

THIS FANTASY IS RELATED TO MANY OTHERS—HE ENJOYMENT OF BEING WATCHED, PERHAPS SOME RESTRAINT, AND CERTAINLY OF BEING "FORCED."

It could involve an Aztec ceremony, where a woman, chosen to be sacrificed, is led to the altar where she's stripped, tied down, and has a variety of sexual acts performed on her.

Other sacrifice fantasy ideas often include variations on this theme: being sacrificed at a black mass (this can be particularly imaginative if you want to include mythological characters, such as the devil) or being prepared and made ready for the pleasure of a king or gangster chief, dressed, and "sacrificed" in whatever style you choose.

CASE STUDY

"MY HUSBAND ONCE PLAYED THIS ROLE WITH ME: I LAY DOWN ON THE TABLE WHILE HE PRETENDED TO BE A PRIEST FROM ANCIENT TIMES, TAKING MY VIRGINITY AS AN OFFERING. IT SOUNDS CRAZY BUT IT WAS SO EROTIC THAT I FELT AS IF THIS WAS MY FIRST TIME. I WAS NERVOUS AND EXCITED. ALTHOUGH HE WAS GENTLE, HE WAS DETACHED TOO, AS IF I REALLY WAS JUST A SACRIFICE. IT WAS SO DIFFERENT TO OUR NORMAL SEX LIFE IT DROVE ME WILD. I FELT AS THOUGH I WAS THE 'CHOSEN ONE,' AND IT INCREASED MY SEXUAL CONFIDENCE BECAUSE I FELT YOUNG AND BEAUTIFUL."

Jane, 35, IT Specialist

4 TALKING **ABOUT FANTASIES**

Talking about fantasies is one of the most intimate things a couple can do. You're allowing each other a tour of your deepest, most private thoughts.

KNOWING WHEN TO TALK (AND WHEN NOT TO) IS VITAL IN THIS SITUATION. A BADLY TIMED CONFESSION CAN RUIN AN ENTIRE RELATIONSHIP BUT, ON THE OTHER HAND, NEVER DISCUSSING YOUR SECRET THOUGHTS CAN MEAN THAT YOU MIGHT NEVER GET TO EXPLORE YOUR SEXUALITY FULLY.

CASE STUDY

"I WANTED TO TELL MY BOYFRIEND ALL ABOUT MY MOST SECRET DESIRES. I WAS WORRIED, THOUGH, BECAUSE EVEN THOUGH I HAVE LESBIAN FANTASIES I'D NEVER WANT TO PUT THEM INTO PRACTICE. I WAITED TILL ONE NIGHT WHEN WE'D BEEN OUT WITH AN ATTRACTIVE FEMALE FRIEND OF MINE, AND THEN I ASKED MY BOYFRIEND WHETHER HE'D EVER CONSIDER A THREESOME. HE SAID THAT EMOTIONALLY HE COULDN'T DO IT, BUT SEXUALLY HE'D LOVE TO. SO I TOLD HIM A STORY, BASED ON MY FANTASY, THAT TURNED US BOTH ON, THOUGH WE KNEW THERE WAS NO DANGER OF IT HAPPENING IN REAL LIFE."

Tracy, 24, Chemist

By talking about fantasies or sharing sexual thoughts aloud, you can tap into each others' desires in a way that touching doesn't allow. It's no use him throwing her around the bed like a wrestler if what she fantasizes about is being gently caressed on a sandy, moonlit beach.

IF HE SECRETLY IMAGINES TAKING
HER FROM BEHIND WHILE SHE
POURS A STREAM OF FILTH FROM
HER LIPS, AND SHE THINKS HE'S
TOO UNADVENTUROUS TO RISK
SUGGESTING ANYTHING KINKY,
THEN THEIR SEX LIFE WILL NEVER
FLOURISH AS IT COULD DO.

THE DIFFICULTY IN TALKING TO YOUR PARTNER IS DEALING WITH THE EMOTIONAL COMPLEXITIES THAT ARISE WHEN SHARING FANTASIES. A FANTASY MIGHT FEEL TOO PERSONAL TO SHARE; OR A FANTASIST MAY BE AFRAID THAT THEIR PARTNER WILL LAUGH OR BE HORRIFIED BY THEM. THEREFORE JUDGING WHAT WILL BE AN EROTIC REVELATION AND WHAT WILL BE THE BEGINNING OF EMBARRASSED SEX IS TOUGH.

If your partner rolls over in bed and murmurs, "What are you thinking?", you'll need to do a quick mental checklist first. Does it involve his or her friends? Does it seem depraved? Can you explain it without losing the eroticism? Do you trust your partner enough to divulge your innermost and secret fantasies?

When To Tell

Assuming you trust your partner, you should certainly explain your fantasies. Your partner can tailor their lovemaking to your mood, understand why certain things turn you on, and therefore communicate directly with your sexual imagination.

THE DOWNSIDE IS OF TELLING IS THAT THE FANTASY CAN OCCASIONALLY BECOME LESS FUN, BECAUSE PART OF FANTASY'S EXCITEMENT IS KNOWING THAT IT'S YOUR SECRET.

CASE STUDY

"I TOLD MY GIRLFRIEND THAT I FANTASIZED ABOUT TYING HER UP, AND IT REALLY UPSET HER. SHE'S QUITE STRAIGHTLACED AND I DON'T THINK SHE'D EVER DO THAT IN REAL LIFE. BUT HER REACTION REALLY PUT ME OFF—EVERY TIME I TRIED TO IMAGINE IT, I IMAGINED HOW SHE FELT AS WELL, WHICH RUINED IT. I HAD TO STOP FOCUSING ON THE FANTASY IN THE END, BECAUSE ONCE I KNEW HOW SHE'D REACT TO THE REALITY, I COULDN'T GET TURNED ON BY IT. I WISH I'D KEPT QUIET."

Laurent, 29, Designer

Never let the listener ask questions unless it is to help elaborate on your fantasy for your pleasure. Remarks such as "But why would all those men be there?" or "So how did you get to be a hooker in the first place, then?" are unhelpful.

You need to be confident that what you're saying is going to be heard and understood. Begin by setting the scene in vague terms if you're unsure of your lover's reaction. Don't say "I'm gyrating on this podium, butt-naked," but instead, say "It takes place in a smoky nightclub." Your lover will need a bit of scene-setting to get in the same mood as you.

BUILDING UP THE ANTICIPATION MAKES A FANTASY MUCH MORE EROTIC, SO CREATE YOUR FANTASY TOGETHER WITH YOUR PARTNER. YOUR PARTNER SHOULD BE SAYING ENCOURAGING WORDS SUCH AS "MM-HMM," "THEN WHAT?," AND "THAT'S VERY INTERESTING...TELL ME MORE." IF THEY LOOK SHY, ENCOURAGE THEM BY ASKING IF THE FANTASY SOUNDS SEXY. IF YOU FEEL THAT THEIR RESPONSE IS BECOMING LESS POSITIVE, THEN YOU DON'T HAVE TO GO ON. YOU MIGHT CHANGE THE SUBJECT AND ASK THEM ABOUT THEIR FANTASY, OR YOU MIGHT EVEN DO THIS BEFORE YOU TALK ABOUT YOURS.

Fantasy that Involves Both of You

Fantasy situations such as "we're on a deserted beach, and the tide's coming in...we're naked, and you pull me onto the sand," etc., are ideal to begin with. They're gentle, harmless, and it's obvious that your partner plays a major role. If that goes down well then you can move on to stories that are a little more raunchy, and you can gently introduce the idea of the dungeon or the principal's office.

If your partner is listening and not laughing, take this as a positive sign, and embellish with truthful details of your own favorite fantasy that stars you both. Even if you think it sounds selfish—"I'm lying down and you're kissing every inch of me..."—tell the story anyway. Your fantasy may chime with a favorite fantasy of your lover, and before you know it you might be enacting the whole thing.

CASE STUDY

"I NEVER WANTED TO TELL MY PARTNER ABOUT MY FAVORITE FANTASY BECAUSE I THOUGHT IT SOUNDED SILLY. IT'S INVOLVES BOTH OF US, IN A HUGE BATH, WITH CANDLES ALL AROUND. HE WASHES ME, AND IT'S HUGELY ROMANTIC. WHEN I CONFESSED, HE REALLY LOVED THE IDEA, AND FOR MY BIRTHDAY HE BOOKED A HOTEL ROOM. THE ROOM WAS LIT BY SCENTED CANDLES AND THE CIRCULAR BATH HAD ROSE PETALS FLOATING ON TOP. IT WAS ABSOLUTELY AMAZING AND I'M SO GLAD I TOLD HIM."

Petra, 23, Mother

Talking About Fantasies just for You

Describing fantasies that don't involve each other can be fraught—introducing another person, however vague, may lead to jealousy. Take time to explain to a potentially jealous partner that this is fantasy, not a world you really want to live in.

If your ideas don't turn your lover on, it doesn't mean there's no point in continuing. Understanding what turns on a lover is halfway to great sex, so it's worth explaining why your fantasy excites you.

FANTASIES WHERE THE WOMAN IS
ON A STAGE, ALONE AND NAKED,
NOT REALIZING THAT SHE'S BEING
WATCHED BY A MAN (HER LOVER), CAN BE
A GOOD STARTING POINT FOR YOUR SHARED
FANTASY. ANY OUTDOOR SITUATION WITH THIS
TYPE OF SCENARIO MIGHT DO. YOUR PARTNER
SHOULD BE ABLE TO RELATE TO THIS FANTASY
AND BE EXCITED BY JOINING IN.

Fantasies about masturbation may turn your partner on and you might introduce further details depending on their reaction. Be aware that most lovers will not want to hear about fantasy characters who are obviously much better looking than them. If you think it's going to make your partner jealous, then you need to explain that you don't consider these characters as real people that you'd want to have a relationship with, but merely as fantasy people in a story.

Things You'd Really Like to Do

Fantasies might be extremely easy to share, or they might be almost impossible, depending on what they are. If your secret wish is to have a threesome, how do you bring it up? In this particular case, you might consider incorporating it within another fantasy and, if your partner responds well, you might move toward the more extreme elements of your fantasy.

The simplest fantasies are those that don't offer the potential for emotional pain, but are just sexual experimentation that you've never dared to explore together until now. Any secret thoughts you've had regarding anal sex, sex in public, or bondage, you can describe in fantasy. Then you can gradually bring them into real life.

CASE STUDY

"I TOLD MY GIRLFRIEND ABOUT THE FANTASY I HAD OF
BEING FOUND MASTURBATING IN THE WOODS BY A
BEAUTIFUL GIRL (I SAID IT WAS HER) AND SHE WAS REALLY
TURNED ON BY IT—SO MUCH SO THAT ONE DAY WE DID
IT FOR REAL. IT WAS A BEAUTIFUL DAY AND I LAY DOWN
ON MY BACK, MASTURBATING, AND SHE CAME AND
'FOUND' ME. SHE DIDN'T LET ME COME BY MY OWN
HAND, SHE WANTED TO DO THAT FOR HERSELF. IT WAS
AN INCREDIBLY EROTIC EXPERIENCE FOR BOTH OF US,
SO I'M REALLY GLAD I CONFESSED."

Stephen, 30, Company Director

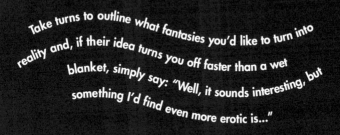

Take turns to outline what fantasies you'd like to turn into reality and, if their idea turns you off faster than a wet blanket, simply say: "Well, it sounds interesting, but something I'd find even more erotic is..."

If you have trouble with words, or feel silly or embarrassed, suggest to your partner that you both write a list of your favorite fantasies in which you appear together, and swap them. If the two differ wildly—"Make love by a riverbank" and "Have an orgy with you and six hookers"—then you should be able to see from your partner's list what they like, and you can adapt your fantasies to include theirs. Then, rewrite both of your lists!

Erotica

A FANTASTICALLY SEXY WAY OF EXPLORING YOUR FANTASIES TOGETHER IS BY USING EROTICA. THERE ARE THOUSANDS OF BOOKS AIMED AT BOTH WOMEN AND MEN WHICH LEAVE NO SEXUAL STONE UNTURNED, SO THERE'S ALMOST CERTAIN TO BE ONE THAT APPEALS TO YOU BOTH.

Pornographic magazines often have short stories in them too, so you could try reading them out loud to each other or, if that feels too embarrassing, then read silently together, while you touch or masturbate each other.

CASE STUDY

"Sometimes we watch porn films together, or I'll read a porn novel before we go to bed—they never fail to put me in the mood. I like historical ones about innocent maidens being corrupted. Sometimes I tell my partner what I've been reading, and we'll pretend to be the characters. Erotica really helps my fantasy life—it's a constant source of new ideas, and it stops us from getting jaded, because there's always something in a book or a movie that we haven't tried yet!"

Dee, 36, Writer

Erotica works brilliantly for women because it stimulates the brain—a very sexual organ! A man will get turned on by erotica but he'll want a real live, naked or lingerie-clad woman to supplement the ideas he's listening to, so dress appropriately.

If your lover reads a few chapters by herself before she goes to bed then it will almost certainly bring her to the exact pitch of sexual excitement that you should be at by just watching her undress. Ask her to tell you what she's read.

Talking Dirty

"Dirty talk" may seem difficult initially, but once you overcome the embarrassment, it's a great way to explore your fantasies or to introduce the idea of role-play without having to bother dressing up.

ONLY "TALK DIRTY" AT A LEVEL YOU'RE COMFORTABLE WITH. IF A WOMAN CAN ONLY JUST MANAGE "PUT IT IN ME" THEN IT'S NO USE YOU EXPECTING TO HEAR, "I WANT YOUR HOT COCK BIG BOY." START YOUR TALK BY SLOWLY AND CAREFULLY DESCRIBING WHAT EACH OTHER IS DOING, AND HOW IT FEELS, BEFORE MOVING ON TO DISCUSS YOUR FANTASIES.

CASE STUDY

"MY HUSBAND AND I LOVE 'TALKING DIRTY'—JUST THINKING ABOUT IT DURING THE DAY AT WORK TURNS ME ON. SOMETIMES I'LL RING HIM AND WHISPER RAUNCHY THINGS DOWN THE PHONE, THEN WE ALWAYS HAVE GREAT SEX WHEN WE GET HOME. I LIKE HIM TO TELL ME STORIES WHILE HE MASTURBATES ME —SOMETIMES ABOUT ME, SOMETIMES ABOUT A FICTIONAL FEMALE—IT DRIVES US BOTH CRAZY WITH DESIRE."

Macy, 26, Social Worker

TOP TEN FANTASIES FOR BOTH OF YOU TO ENJOY

1. Having sex somewhere unusual, for example, on the banks of a lake

2. Watching each other masturbate

3. Dressing each other in sexy clothes

4. The male partner as a macho man, such as a fireman, or Indiana Jones

5. The female partner as a seductive and powerful sex goddess
6. Having sex in a public place
7. Romance: bathing together in rose petals, four-poster beds, sharing champagne, etc.
8. Film scenes
9. Making pornographic movies
10. Master- or mistress-and-slave roles

"Talking dirty" works best if you talk in the present tense: "I'm on a bed and you come in... you're naked and you've got a huge erection..." and describe what you imagine is happening, moment by moment. Guys can start off with "You're lying down naked and you look unbelieveably sexy." However, in your excitement, be careful not to veer too far off a fantasy that suits both of you!

5 ROLE-PLAY

Role-play is just a form of "grown-up" play. It's fun and frivolous, and can lead to great sex. Role-play takes away the pressure of being yourselves, worrying about the kids or work, and gives you the chance to "act" like someone else—usually someone very sexy indeed.

Pretending to be another character can help you to lose your inhibitions and let you enjoy experiences that you might never have tried otherwise. Both men and women can gain huge pleasure from dressing up and imagining they're a doctor and nurse, strangers, or whoever they feel like being.

CASE STUDY

"MY BOYFRIEND AND I LOVE TO DRESS UP AND PLAY ROLES: I'LL BE SUBMISSIVE, THE NURSE TO HIS DOCTOR; OR WE'LL REVERSE THE ROLES, AND I'LL PUT ON A BLACK LEATHER BASQUE AND DEMAND SEXUAL FAVORS. ROLE-PLAY BRINGS OUT DIFFERENT SIDES TO OUR SEXUALITY. HE DOESN'T HAVE TO WONDER ABOUT PICKING UP A HOOKER BECAUSE I CAN PRETEND TO BE ONE, AND I DON'T HAVE TO FANTASIZE ABOUT A SEXY ROCK STAR, BECAUSE I CAN BELIEVE HE REALLY IS ONE."

Bernadette, 31, Chef

CASE STUDY

"MY FANTASY WAS TO BE DEFLOWERED IN FRONT OF A CROWD, AND MY HUSBAND SUGGESTED WE SHOULD TRY PRETENDING. WE TRIED IT IN OUR BEDROOM, BUT IT DIDN'T WORK—THE SURROUNDINGS WERE TOO FAMILIAR. A FEW DAYS LATER, HE SAID WE SHOULD TRY OUTSIDE. I WAS NERVOUS BUT EXCITED AND WE DROVE OUT TO A NEARBY HILL. PARTLY CONCEALED BY A ROCK, WE TRIED THE FANTASY AGAIN. I COULD FEEL THE BREEZE ON MY BODY, AND EASILY IMAGINE THERE WERE CROWDS WATCHING AT THE FOOT OF THE HILL. IT WAS THE BEST ORGASM I EVER HAD."

Georgia, 48, Set Designer

YOU CAN ACT OUT A FANTASY THAT APPEALS
TO ONE OF YOU AND NOT THE OTHER, BUT
THIS ISN'T MUCH FUN. HOW CAN YOU EXPECT
YOUR PARTNER TO BE ENTHUSIASTIC ABOUT
PLAYING A ROLE THEY CLEARLY AREN'T TURNED
ON BY? TALK ABOUT YOUR FANTASIES WITH
YOUR PARTNER UNTIL YOU FIND SOMETHING
THAT YOU BOTH ENJOY.

The "best laid plans of mice and men" often go astray. Although you both need to be convinced of what you're doing in a role-play situation, remember to retain a sense of humor in case things don't work out the way you expected. And don't be discouraged if things do go wrong—try again, or try something different next time.

Make or buy yourself a prop box—otherwise, you might find yourself running around the house trying to find a feather duster and an apron before you go off the boil. Include anything that might help your dressing up fantasies in your box.

CASE STUDY

"WE KEEP A SPECIAL 'RAUNCHY BOX' UNDER THE BED—IT'S LIKE A DRESSING-UP BOX, WITH AN ASSORTMENT OF PROPS WE'VE COLLECTED OVER THE YEARS TO HELP US ACT OUT OUR FANTASY SCENARIOS. IT'S ALWAYS FUN AND EXCITING WHEN WE GET IT OUT. JENNY HAS A PVC MAID COSTUME, AND I HAVE A BLINDFOLD AND HANDCUFFS FOR HER DOMINATION FANTASIES. THERE'S ALL KINDS OF STUFF IN THERE, BECAUSE WE'VE FOUND THAT REALLY GETTING INTO CHARACTER CAN HELP US LET GO AND BE SEXUAL WITH ONE ANOTHER."

Adam, 34, Engineer

TOP TEN PROPS

1. HANDCUFFS FOR BONDAGE GAMES.

2. APRON AND WHITE HAT FOR A FRENCH MAID OR NURSE

3. WHITE BABY-DOLL OUTFIT, FOR THE VIRGIN IN YOU

4. POLICEMAN'S HAT

5. FEATHER DUSTER

6. NOTEPAD AND GLASSES, FOR A POLICEMAN OR A "BUSINESS INTERVIEW"

7. BLACK "TOUGH LADY" KNEE-LENGTH BOOTS

8. SUIT FOR AN ALL-PURPOSE AUTHORITY FIGURE

9. CANE OR SMALL WHIP FOR NAUGHTY BOYS AND GIRLS

10. BLINDFOLD OF BLACK SILK OR LEATHER

DECIDE IN ADVANCE WHAT YOUR
FANTASY IS GOING TO BE.
IF YOU MAKE IT UP AS YOU GO
ALONG, NEITHER WILL KNOW THE
TONE OR THE INTENTION (A GENTLE
SEDUCTION, OR RED HOT SEX?).
AGREE A BASIC SCENARIO AND, IF
YOU WANT TO, YOU COULD
EVEN WRITE A SCRIPT.

STORY

A wealthy lady lies on her bed of silk sheets, within her modern mansion. She's had a long bath and passes the time by playing with herself. The butler knocks on the door and, without waiting, enters the room. The lady pretends to be shocked, telling him that his behavior is inexcusable. Although he apologises, it's obvious that the sight of the lady's flesh stirs him. The lady tells him that, since he has barged in and likes what he sees, he might as well touch her. Nervously, he runs his hands over her soft, warm body, touching her breasts. Becoming more confident he touches her clitoris. "No, No!" she says, "Not like that—you must use your tongue." He is the servant, so he must obey.

ROLE-PLAY CAN TAKE PLACE ANYWHERE IN THE HOUSE, BUT TRY TO SUIT THE ENVIRONMENT TO THE FANTASY. SO, IF THE GAME IS "MAID AND MASTER," TRY THE KITCHEN, OR FOR A BUSINESS INTERVIEW, DO IT IN YOUR HOME OFFICE. THE BEDROOM IS MULTIPURPOSE OF COURSE, BUT NOT QUITE SO EXCITING.

A hotel room is a great place for fantasy sex—it's anonymous and you can pretend to be anyone. An interesting role-play is to check in separately and meet in the bar as strangers. Ask each other questions, making them as sexy and saucy as you dare. (You might have assumed different characters and names in advance.) As you flirt and "get to know each other," you can invite your "pick-up" back to your room for some great sex.

CASE STUDY

"MY BOYFRIEND AND I DROVE SEPARATELY TO A FOUR-STAR HOTEL. DAVE CHECKED IN FIRST, AND I ARRIVED AN HOUR LATER. I SPOTTED HIM IN THE BAR, AND ASKED IF I COULD JOIN HIM. HE BOUGHT A DRINK AND WE CHATTED, LIKE POLITE STRANGERS. AFTER A FEW DRINKS, HE PUT HIS HAND ON MY LEG AND WHISPERED 'I FIND YOU VERY ATTRACTIVE.' IT WAS A SURPRISING TURN-ON. HE SUGGESTED WE GO TO HIS ROOM. I COULD SEE THE OTHER CUSTOMERS STARING, THINKING I WAS A PUSHOVER. WE STARTED KISSING IN THE ELEVATOR AND WERE DESPERATE FOR EACH OTHER BY THE TIME WE GOT TO THE ROOM."

Dagmar, 35, Artist

Role-play gives you all the fun of polygamy too, without the messy misery of extra-marital affairs. And while there is some role-play that would only work for a few of us, there are certain scenes that are exciting to most couples. Choose the fantasy that appeals, and enjoy your new selves.

Schoolgirl

This is a favorite fantasy because of the contrast between innocence and authority —the "schoolgirl and teacher" is therefore worth having a go at. The woman plays a teenage pupil with a rebellious streak—this may take the form of a sexy uniform or being rude to the "teacher." He (the teacher) tells her off, and afterward comes punishment, discipline, or seduction—or all three!

Schoolboy

THE FEMALE BECOMES THE "SEXY TEACHER" AND THE MAN IS A "NAUGHTY SCHOOLBOY." THE SCHOOLBOY IS, OF COURSE, OLD ENOUGH TO REALLY BE VERY NAUGHTY. THIS CAN GO THE WAY OF PUNISHMENT OR SEDUCTION, OR BOTH. IT'LL FEEL VERY AROUSING BECAUSE HE FULFILS AN "OLDER WOMAN" FANTASY, AND SHE BREAKS A TABOO IN SEDUCING A YOUNG ADMIRER WITH WHOM SHE SHOULDN'T HAVE ANYTHING TO DO.

CASE STUDY

"I FIND THIS IDEA A REAL TURN ON. IT REMINDS ME OF WHEN I FIRST BECAME AWARE OF MY SEXUALITY AS A TEENAGER, SURROUNDED BY SCHOOLGIRLS IN SHORT SKIRTS. I DRESS AS AN OLD-FASHIONED HEADMASTER AND STAND AT THE DESK WITH A PILE OF "MARKING." I TURN TO MY GIRLFRIEND, WHO IS DRESSED AS A NAUGHTY SCHOOLGIRL WITH HER SHIRT BUTTONS UNDONE TO SHOW OFF HER BRA.

I ASK HER A QUESTION AND SHE GETS IT WRONG, SO I SUMMON HER TO MY DESK, INSTRUCT HER TO BEND OVER, AND GIVE HER A GOOD SPANKING. I CONTINUE TO ASK HER QUESTIONS, AND EVERY TIME SHE GETS ONE WRONG, I GET MORE RISQUÉ. I PULL DOWN HER PANTIES, OR CARESS HER BACKSIDE, UNTIL IT ENDS WITH ME HAVING SEX WITH HER ACROSS THE DESK. IT'S A VERY NORMAL FANTASY BUT IT WORKS FOR US EVERY TIME."

Tim, 40, Advertising Creative

Maid and Master

The "maid and master" fantasy can take many forms but there's usually an element of submission involved. The maid innocently bends over and the master sneakily caresses her thighs, then puts his hand between her legs. Or else he stands over her while she completes little tasks that he's set, such as making a cup of tea. He'll find fault with what she is doing and decide that she must be punished.

Alternatively, the "maid" might be wicked and have no respect for the "master"; while she's supposed to be polishing the room, she might flick his penis with the feather duster. He isn't supposed to be excited by her, but she teases him until he can't take any more.

Strangers

This role-play is eternally popular for providing all the thrill of infidelity without actually straying. The "stranger" fantasy has a variety of possibilities, from two people meeting in a park and going back to the house in silence to have sex (and you can do that for real very easily) to meeting in a bar, following each other to a train, then heading for the restroom to have fast, frantic sex.

If you're at home, masks are an ideal prop—you could be dancers at a Venetian masked ball or members of an S&M club. But the idea that your identities are concealed from each other is highly arousing and frees you to do and say outrageous, sexy things that you might otherwise never consider.

Business Interview

The ultimate power-play, a "business interview" can cast either of you in the role of interviewer (wearing a suit and glasses), firing questions at a nervous "interviewee." Use questions such as "Can you give us a practical demonstration of your interpersonal skills?" A stern interview manner is essential, but this should gradually crumble as you are seduced by the sexy and attractive interviewee. Alternatively, the interviewer can beckon the interviewee over to tell them what they have to do to get the "job."

Domination

Props for this might include handcuffs, a whip, and a blindfold, or any combination of these. One of you is the "slave," who is forced to do the other's bidding. This might mean that the slave is ordered to give their "master" or "mistress" a massage or, if you like your pleasure with a bit of pain, the naughty slave might need to be spanked. You will gradually work your way toward having sex. How you do it is up to you!

TAKING TURNS IS A GOOD IDEA IN THIS ROLE-PLAY, SO THAT YOU CAN BOTH ENJOY BEING IN CONTROL.

Celebrities

YOU CAN PRETEND THAT THE WOMAN IS A GROUPIE
VISITING A ROCK STAR AFTER A GIG, OR A FAN VISITING
A FILM SET WHO MANAGES TO SEDUCE THE STAR
IN THEIR TRAILER. SUNGLASSES ARE A FUN PROP
FOR THIS ONE. IF YOU'RE A FEMALE "STAR" YOU
CAN LOOK AS GLAMOROUS AS YOU LIKE,
WITH FULL MAKEUP AND A FAKE FUR COAT.

You can play the role of a real star, but be aware of
jealousy—if she's moaning "Brad! Brad!" or he's
whispering "Oh, Julia!" then it may not be the
experience either of you hoped for.

Doctors and Nurses

This old favorite works every time. There are a number of variations on this particular theme: Hot doctor and sexy nurse; patient and sexy nurse; patient and sexy doctor. You might even like to make up some symptoms that need to be "personally" treated, such as "sex addiction." Include lines like "Where does it hurt?" and "I'll have to get closer to have a proper look." Props can include anything that you can probe with.

Hooker and John

A SLEAZY FANTASY CAN BE GOOD FUN IF
THE WOMAN IS PREPARED TO DRESS UP LIKE
A HOOKER (THINK JULIA ROBERTS IN *PRETTY
WOMAN*, WITH THIGH LENGTH BOOTS AND A
GLAMOROUS MINI-DRESS), NEGOTIATE SEX, AND
ARRANGE A PRICE. FOR AUTHENTICITY, MONEY
MUST BE PAID.

Swap roles in the above "hooker and john" scenario: he
can become the woman's "male escort" for the night.

Movie Characters

Acting out movie love scenes is highly erotic.
Directors find the sexiest ideas and, if they've
done all the hard work for you, why turn
down to chance to try it out yourself? Choose
a movie that you've both seen and try
enacting scenes from it (remember $9^1/_2$
Weeks?), or, just take on the personality of
the character. For example, you might be
Bruce Willis in Die Hard (you'd be a man's
man, saving his woman).

Voyeurs

Playing the role of being watched by others can be highly erotic, and requires no props at all. She undresses, or masturbates, pretending that she is unaware of his presence, while he watches through the door of the bedroom (which has been left ajar). The man may also want to film her on a camcorder.

The positions can be reversed as she "spies" on him while he masturbates. You can use mirrors so that he can see her doing this.

6 ALTERNATIVE **FANTASY**

It isn't abnormal to consider your fantasies bizarre; but they may be much more common than you think. You only have to look at Nancy Friday's books on fantasy (*My Secret Garden* and *Women on Top*) to understand that anything goes— these normal women and men dream of everything, from sex with their sister to excitement with a German Shepherd.

It may come as a shock to recognize that images of animals or pain turn you on, but remember: in your mind, there are no barriers to sexual stimulation.

293

CASE STUDY

"I'M LYING ON MY BACK ON THE BED, NAKED, WHEN A HUGE DOBERMAN DOG COMES INTO THE ROOM, AND JUMPS ONTO THE BED. AT FIRST I'M SCARED BECAUSE IT'S SO HUGE, BUT IT STARTS TO SNIFF ME ALL OVER AND, AFTER A WHILE, I REALIZE I'M BECOMING TURNED ON BY ITS COLD, WET NOSE PROBING ME. IT LICKS ME OCCASIONALLY, AND I GET REALLY EXCITED. THEN IT BEGINS TO SNIFF AND LICK BETWEEN MY LEGS. IT CARRIES ON DOING THAT UNTIL I COME; THEN IT THRUSTS ITS HUGE ERECTION INSIDE ME, VIOLENTLY."

Sarah, 32, Real Estate Agent

ALTHOUGH SOME FANTASIES SEEM SPECIALIST, THEY WILL ALMOST CERTAINLY BE INCORPORATED WITH OTHER FANTASIES. FANTASIES THAT INVOLVE FETISHISM CAN BE ABOUT A PERSON YOU'D LIKE TO HAVE SEX WITH, BUT THEY MIGHT ALSO INVOLVE VOYEURISM, WHERE THE FETISH OBJECT IS BEING WORN OR HELD BY A PERSON BEING WATCHED.

Many ideas have been explored by erotic literature —there's very little that hasn't been discussed or fictionalized. Check out the *Encyclopedia of Unusual Sex Practices* by Brenda Love for an overview.

TOP TEN ALTERNATIVE FANTASIES

1. ANIMALS

2. ALIENS

3. PAIN

4. FETISH

5. VOYEURISM

6. INCEST

7. TERROR

8. GOLDEN SHOWERS

9. TRANSEXUALISM

10. ADULT BABIES

SOME FANTASIES ARE A WAY OF ABANDONING SEXUAL INHIBITION, HOWEVER SHY OR RESERVED YOU ARE IN REALITY. THEY ALLOW YOU TO ENJOY SHOCKINGLY OPEN FANTASIES ABOUT THINGS THAT MIGHT SEEM UNACCEPTABLE. THEY CONNECT YOU WITH YOUR DEEPER SEXUAL PSYCHE, AND ALLOW YOU THE FREEDOM TO EXPLORE IT WITHOUT ANY FEAR OF DISAPPROVAL.

There are many reasons why fantasies away from the norm can be a turn-on. It's true that taboo subjects are sexy, because knowing that something is considered bad by society, or by parents, can give you the illicit thrill associated with sexual feelings. To know that your secret thoughts would shock others heightens your arousal.

CASE STUDY

"I HAVE NEVER HAD SEX WITH AN ANIMAL AND I NEVER WOULD, BUT ONCE WHEN I WAS YOUNGER, MY CAT LICKED MY NIPPLE AND IT UNEXPECTEDLY GAVE ME A REAL THRILL. SINCE THEN, I HAVE HAD FANTASIES ABOUT ANIMALS, PARTICULARLY THE IDEA OF HAVING SEX WITH A BIG CAT, LIKE A TIGER, WITH THE HUGE POWER IT HAS AND THE FACT THAT IT COULD KILL ME AT ANY MOMENT. I IMAGINE IT TAKING ME FROM BEHIND, WHILE I AM ON ALL FOURS. I IMAGINE IT WOULD HAVE AN ENORMOUS ERECTION AND HOLD THE BACK OF MY NECK, VERY LIGHTLY IN ITS JAWS, WHILE WE HAD SEX."

Susie, 28, Editor

Animals

For people who have witnessed animals mating, the sheer sexual urgency of it can be highly arousing. Watching a stallion mate with a mare or two dogs having sex is exciting because they aren't bound by any social codes. Animals procreate in public happily, and display their erections and arousal without shame.

FANTASY SEX WITH ANIMALS CAN BE APPEALING BECAUSE IT IS JUST PURE SEX. IT ALLOWS YOU TO REDISCOVER YOUR "NAKED," ANIMAL NATURE.

TOP FIVE FANTASY ANIMALS

1. Dogs
2. Horses
3. Snakes
4. Big cats
5. Gorillas and monkeys

CASE STUDY

"I ONCE SAW A GORILLA MASTURBATING AT THE ZOO, AND I WAS SHOCKED THAT IT REALLY TURNED ME ON. IT HAD NO EMBARRASSMENT AND ACTUALLY SEEMED QUITE PROUD AS IT DISPLAYED ITS PENIS TO EVERYONE. SINCE THEN, I'VE SOMETIMES THOUGHT ABOUT IT WHEN I'VE BEEN MASTURBATING, AND IT'S REALLY DRIVEN ME WILD. I WISH HUMANS COULD BE MORE OPEN ABOUT THEIR SEXUALITY—NOT NECESSARILY PUTTING IT ON DISPLAY, BUT IN TERMS OF PRIDE IN THEIR ABILITY TO ORGASM, EVEN ALONE. I ENJOY THE THOUGHT OF THAT GORILLA, AND I DON'T FEEL GUILTY AT ALL."

Emma, 32, Riding Instructor

For women, being taken by a large animal is a fantasy about losing control and a longing to be ultimately desirable, to everybody and everything. Inhibitions are lost with an animal in a way that is impossible with a sentient human being.

Most animals that are fantasy partners are large and/or powerful—few people fantasize about mice. Tigers, gorillas, and German Shepherds are large and dangerous and therefore potentially erotic, because the power that lies with them, both physically and sexually, provides a thrill.

CASE STUDY

"I'VE ALWAYS LOVED HORSES AND RIDING AND, WHILE IN REALITY I'VE NEVER WANTED TO HAVE SEX WITH ONE, I HAVE IMAGINED IT. I LOVE THE IDEA OF ITS WARMTH AND HUGENESS, AND HOW IT WOULD ENCLOSE ME. I THINK ABOUT BEING REALLY GENTLE, AND IT BARELY NOTICING ME BEHIND. IT'S A FANTASY ABOUT SOMETHING BIGGER THAN ME THAT EXPECTS NOTHING IN RETURN—IT'S QUITE A COMFORTING FANTASY, IN A STRANGE WAY."

Paul, 34, Surveyor

STORY

Alone in a room, a naked woman is lying on a bed with a boa-type snake. She puts out her hand to touch the snake's skin, and finds it is dry and smooth. She lies down next to it, and allows it to slither up and down her body. The snake inserts its tail inside her vagina, flicking it back and forth against her, and then slips it out to brush over her clitoris. All the time the rest of the snake coils all over the woman's body, inside and out, as she moans with pleasure.

Incest

Incest is the ultimate taboo. However, if you really don't have any natural urges toward this kinds of fantasy, then don't force yourself—obviously it doesn't turn you on. If you do feel something, then you needn't feel guilty—it's only in your head, and in some people's minds, fantasizing is not such a terrible thing. You can have as much or as little fun with it as you like.

STORY

Relaxing in the bath full of bubbles, a woman restlessly washes her body. Her half-brother walks in on her, and immediately apologizes. Not caring, she asks him to stay and chat. As they talk, he absent-mindedly picks up the sponge and starts to squeeze water over her back and then her breasts. She invites him to get in, and he does so. He soaps his hands and gently washes her breasts, and between her legs. She massages his penis under the water, both of them sighing with pleasure, until eventually they both come.

Many films explore incest, and not always in the horrified, negative way that you might expect. For example, the innocent Luke and Leia enjoy a chaste kiss in *Star Wars* and *The Empire Strikes Back*, and Rob Lowe and Jodie Foster enjoy an erotic but fun sibling affair in *Hotel New Hampshire*.

CASE STUDY

"MY SISTER IS A LESBIAN AND, IN MY FANTASY, SHE'S IN BED WITH HER GIRLFRIEND, WHO'S VERY ATTRACTIVE. I WALK IN AND THEY BREAK OFF KISSING AND ASK WHAT I WANT. I TELL THEM I WANT TO WATCH. THEY AGREE, AND I SIT FACING THE BED WHILE THEY GET OFF WITH EACH OTHER. AFTER A WHILE, HER GIRLFRIEND ASKS ME IF I'D LIKE TO JOIN IN. IT'S SO TABOO AND EROTIC. I GET IN BETWEEN THEM, AND WE ALL FONDLE AND CARESS EACH OTHER. ONE OF THEM GIVES ME A BLOW-JOB, AND WE ALL COME TOGETHER."

Jason, 29, Construction Worker

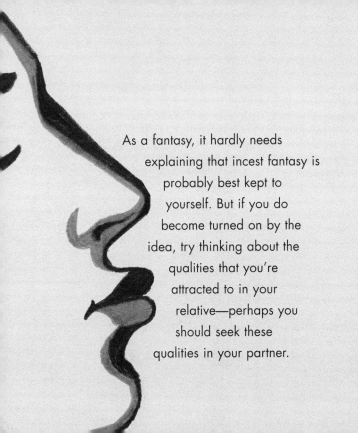

As a fantasy, it hardly needs explaining that incest fantasy is probably best kept to yourself. But if you do become turned on by the idea, try thinking about the qualities that you're attracted to in your relative—perhaps you should seek these qualities in your partner.

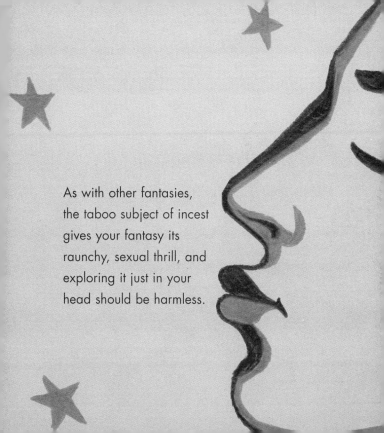

As with other fantasies, the taboo subject of incest gives your fantasy its raunchy, sexual thrill, and exploring it just in your head should be harmless.

S&M (Pain)

THE PLEASURE/PAIN PRINCIPLE—THAT IS, INFLICTING
PAIN AS WELL AS RECEIVING IT—FORMS THE BASIS
OF THIS FANTASY. IT TENDS TO CENTER ON GIVING
UP CONTROL AND ALLOWING SOMEONE TO
"ABUSE" YOU THROUGH INFLICTING PAIN ON YOU.
OR, YOU MIGHT PREFER TO BE THE ABUSER.

As with all fantasies, there is more involvement than
just the basic "pain." You'll have different settings in
your fantasy and within them, perhaps, some
bondage. Choose a dominant or submissive role,
depending on your preference.

STORY

Spreadeagled on a table in a dungeon, a man stiffens when his mistress comes in. She is wearing tight, black clothes and carrying a whip. She struts over to the man and tells him he's about to be punished. She cracks the whip down over his thighs, and trails the tip over his erect penis. The man grimaces with the pain, which excites him more. She is also turned on by punishing him. She turns him over and whips his buttocks, and shouts abuse at him. Secretly she wants him. The man gets up and takes the woman from behind, over the table. The woman is wild with lust, and climaxes violently.

"Pain" might be relatively light, such as a man slapping your bottom for being naughty. For the boys, it might be a sexy lady "schoolteacher" slapping a naughty "schoolboy." More extreme pain might be similar to the "Joan of Arc" story on page 333. It might even feature a man on a "rack," being tortured with hot pokers.

The thrill in "pain" can be in the idea of the pain itself. Spanking, whipping, and clamping nipples can happen within everyday sex. In fantasy, you have the opportunity to extend this type of "agony" through your imagination, to include huge machines developed specifically for torturing you.

STORY

A scantily-clad woman is tied to a stake, like Joan of Arc. She is being burned for witchcraft, and the flames are leaping around her. Crowds of people are watching, cheering whenever she screams as the fire burns her arms and legs. Suddenly a man bursts through the crowd. He plunges through the flames and swiftly pulls the woman out. The crowd can now see that she is a beautiful woman, not an ugly, old witch, and they turn on her persecutors. The woman is so glad to be alive that she falls to her knees, offering herself to her rescuer. He grabs her and they have wild, abandoned sex right in front of everyone.

TOP TEN S&M (PAIN) FANTASIES

1. WHIPPING

2. SLAPPING

3. PADDLES

4. CLOTHES STUDDED ON THE INSIDE, OR THAT ARE TIGHT AND UNCOMFORTABLE

5. BRANDING WITH HOT IRONS

6. BITING

7. SCRATCHING

8. HANDCUFFS AND BINDINGS

9. CUTTING

10. CUSTOM-MADE TORTURE EQUIPMENT

In fantasy the pain is not real; the idea of pain and your helplessness mixes with the sexual stimulation provided by the fantasy, which adds up to your having a very sexy time.

YOU PROBABLY KNOW WHAT TURNS
YOU ON, FROM BOOKS THAT
YOU'VE READ, OR FILMS THAT
YOU'VE SEEN WHERE YOU BECOME
STIMULATED WHEN WATCHING A
PARTICULAR SCENE. DON'T BE
AFRAID TO INCORPORATE THESE
IDEAS INTO YOUR FANTASIES.

Fetish

Fetishism is much more common among men than women. Recently fetishism has come to suggest wearing rubber or the styles associated with S&M. But a fetish can refer to any object of arousal, from shoes or large breasts to rubber sheets.

Arousal and orgasm have become so closely linked to fetishism that sex without an object of desire might lack intensity, or even be impossible. Again, it will often be part of a scenario that includes other types of fantasy.

STORY

A man is licking a woman's very, very high-heeled shoes all over. She is wearing nothing else, and the shoes have leather straps that tie tightly around her ankles and legs. The smell of the leather permeates the air, and the man begins to lick her perfumed skin too. Her skin is soft and warm in contrast with the point of the shoe, which is vicious and sharp. She lifts the spike of a heel and presses it against the man's skin, and massages the man's penis with the side of it, which drives him mad with pleasure. He grasps the woman and enters her from above, her legs wrapped around his head.

SOME FANTASY FETISHES CAN BE HIGHLY AROUSING. HIGH HEELS ARE THE MOST COMMON AROUSAL TOOLS BECAUSE THEY SUGGEST A TORTURE OF THE FOOT (AND THE FOOT ITSELF MIGHT BE A FETISH OBJECT). THEY MAKE THE WEARER WALK WITH A SWAY, AND MANY SHOE-FANCIERS CLAIM THAT THE SMELL OF LEATHER IS NOT DISSIMILAR TO A WOMAN'S SECRETIONS.

Rubber is tight-fitting, and contours the body smoothly. Its association with "hard" sex makes it a turn-on for many. Rubber is warm to the touch, like a second skin; and the combination of its texture and smell can be a real turn-on.

CASE STUDY

"I have a fetish about fur. It doesn't have to be real but it has to feel real against my skin. I think it comes from when I was young, and my mother had a fur coat. When she held me in it, I felt so warm and safe. I fantasize about women in fur coats with nothing underneath; I'd love to lie on a fur rug to have sex. It gives me a frisson of excitement just to touch and run my hands over fur."

Simon, 23, Sales Executive

CERTAIN PEOPLE BECOME EROTICALLY AROUSED BY HAIR OF A PARTICULAR LENGTH OR COLOR. THEY ONLY FANCY BLONDES OR REDHEADS—SOME EVEN BEG THEIR PARTNERS TO DYE THEIR HAIR.

Some men prefer a certain hairstyle. If their fantasy is the "schoolteacher," they may be aroused by hair worn in a tight bun or for a "schoolgirl," braids. Severe hairstyles—tightly pulled back ponytails, for example—have a hint of S&M about them.

ANOTHER POPULAR FETISH IS FOR FINGERNAILS. A GUY WILL HAVE LEARNED TO ASSOCIATE SEXUAL FEELINGS WITH LONG, POLISHED NAILS, AND BECOMES TURNED ON BY THE IDEA OF SEEING THEM AS SHE GIVES HIM A HAND-JOB, OR STROKES HIM.

Certain parts of the body appeal to fetishists, particularly feet. He may want to simply kiss and caress attractive feet or it may go so far that he wants to ejaculate on them while she wears high-heeled leather shoes. Breasts are another focus—some men can only become turned on by women with large breasts.

Aliens

NONHUMANS FEATURE HIGHLY IN ALTERNATIVE
FANTASIES. OTHER VERSIONS OF THE "ALIEN"
FANTASY MIGHT INCLUDE WIZARDS OR WITCHES,
ANGELS, OR GHOSTS. DON'T BE AFRAID TO LET
YOUR IMAGINATION ROAM FULLY AROUND THE
PLETHORA OF POSSIBILITIES.

In fantasy, the "alien" can take you to a spacecraft or
another planet where social codes are different, and make
you do all sorts of raunchy things. Because your "alien"
can look any way you want, it's really easy to adapt the
fantasy—from being forced into sex with a really grotesque
creature to being seduced by a very attractive nonhuman.

STORY

Driving home from work, a woman is stopped in her car by a beam of light. She gets out and sees a large spaceship, from which half human-sized creatures, with two blank eyes, are emerging. They beckon for her to come inside the ship. Once she's in, they strap her down onto a table. Her clothes are stripped off with lasers, and the alien creatures begin to probe her. They want to know what an orgasm is, and they apply a terribly powerful vibrator between the woman's legs, and wait to record her response. She is incredibly aroused, and they are startled by how strongly she reacts. The woman has an enormous orgasm, and the aliens choose to keep her captive for further experiments.

7 INSPIRATION AND **REALITY**

Fantasy is not limited only to the imagination. There's no reason why both of you can't enjoy the same fantasy inspirations—either by reading aloud, by talking during sex, or by acting out roles.

Fantasy needs triggers that work for both men and women, so think carefully about whether your fantasy will not just turn you on, but your partner as well.

Books

Inspiration for your fantasy can come from books or visual sources, such as soft porn movies or erotic films. Or it can be interactive, such as using texts found in internet chatrooms.

Women's sexual imagination is often better activated by erotic writing than pictures. A story offers far more scope for her to embellish or add to the sexual elements of the story that appeal to her most. However, this means that she can add exciting roles for men when it comes to doing it for real.

There are various book imprints that focus on sexual stories for women—although men read them too. One of the best known is the internationally sold "Black Lace" series, which offers a huge range of sexual scenarios in novel form. The stories can be anything from "racy" to what some might consider as pornographic.

CASE STUDY

"READING MY FIRST EROTIC NOVEL REALLY CHANGED MY OUTLOOK ON WOMEN'S PORN. I THOUGHT IT WAS ALL TACKY, BUT THIS STORY HAD A GREAT PLOT, AND WAS SO EROTIC I COULD HARDLY WAIT TO READ MORE. IT WAS ABOUT A WOMAN STAYING IN A CASTLE RUN BY A MYSTERIOUS, SEXUALLY UNINHIBITED GUY. THERE WAS SEX ON ALMOST EVERY PAGE: WITH MEN, WOMEN, AND GROUPS. AFTER MOST CHAPTERS I ENDED UP MASTURBATING AND, BECAUSE I WAS SINGLE AT THE TIME, IT MADE ME FEEL MORE ALIVE."

Jenny, 26, Office Manager

Books, or better still short stories, can be read alone, but it's much more fun to read with your partner. Turn your bedroom into a boudoir using scented candles, low-lights, silky sheets, and, of course, your "toy box," and take turns reading aloud to each other. It might be fun to speak the lines, but just reading the text aloud will stimulate your imagination.

If you want to play the roles, copy the sexual activities of the books. You won't be able to do this exactly, of course, but you can stay within the theme of the book so, for example, if the heroine is being tied to a rack, then tie your lover to the bed.

The woman might go to bed earlier than the man, reading a few chapters before he arrives in their bedroom. She will have lots of sexy ideas for fantasies to inspire her while they make love. She might make up fantasies for him to enjoy too as she goes.

STORY

A couple are in bed together, and the woman reads aloud to her boyfriend from a book she has bought. It's a really sexy story about a man and a woman exploring all the possible ways they could make love—really passionate and quite dirty. The man begins to caress the woman's uncovered breasts, as she reads a passage about how the couple try every sexual position possible. He suggests they do the same, using lots of lubrication. Groaning with ecstacy, in a tumble of bedclothes, passion, and excitement, they finally reach the height of their climax together.

You can use the characters from
erotic novels to inspire fantasies of
your own to share with your partner,
incorporating them into your lovemaking
or enjoying them as role-play.
Dressing and acting as the characters from
a story can be highly arousing, even if you
don't stick to the script!

COMMON THEMES IN EROTIC NOVELS INCLUDE:
INNOCENCE CORRUPTED; HISTORICAL SETTINGS;
MAIDS AND NUNS; FEISTY WOMEN AND
DANGEROUS MEN; ORGIES; BISEXUALITY;
AND ALSO VOYEURISM.

THE BOOKS ARE WELL RESEARCHED TO ECHO
COMMON FANTASIES. BUT IF THAT KIND OF
WRITING DOESN'T APPEAL, TRY SOME CLASSIC
LITERARY EROTICA INSTEAD.

TOP 5 EROTIC BOOKS

1. *DELTA OF VENUS*, ANAÏS NIN

2. *FANNY HILL*, JOHN CLELAND

3. *MOLL FLANDERS*, DANIEL DEFOE

4. *FEAR OF FLYING*, ERICA JONG

5. *LADY CHATTERLEY'S LOVER*, D.H. LAWRENCE

CASE STUDY

"I ALWAYS ADORED *LADY CHATTERLEY'S LOVER*. RECENTLY, MY HUSBAND AND I READ THE SEXIEST PASSAGES ALOUD TO EACH OTHER. THEN HE PUT ON AN OLD WAISTCOAT AND COLLARLESS SHIRT, WHILE I WORE A TWINSET AND PEARLS AND SOME SILK PANTIES. WE GIGGLED A LOT, BUT IT WAS REALLY EXCITING. WE DIDN'T HAVE ANY FORGET-ME-NOTS FOR MY PUBIC HAIR, BUT I REALLY LOST MYSELF IN IT. I HAD THE BEST ORGASM EVER!"

Angela, 30, Sculptor

Magazines

Porn magazines are often the first experience that boys have of seeing naked women. For this reason, magazines can hold a special place in their hearts. Although women may not feel the same about them, sharing magazines can render them far less threatening, turning them from male-only entertainment into a thrill for both of you.

Your magazine doesn't have to be a "porno mag." You might find fetish clubs, for example, that produce their own magazines. These will give you ideas that you can incorporate in your fantasies.

THERE ARE MANY DIFFERENT TYPES OF
PORNOGRAPHIC MAGAZINES FOR YOU AND
YOUR PARTNER TO ENJOY—MAGAZINES WITH
PICTURES OF SCANTILY-CLAD BLONDES WITH
UNNATURALLY LARGE BREASTS ARE NOT THE
ONLY ONES AVAILABLE. MANY MAGAZINES
SPECIALIZE IN DIFFERENT SUBJECTS: RAUNCHY
SCHOOLGIRLS, COWGIRLS, BONDAGE,
FETISHISM, OR ORGIES.

CASE STUDY

"THERE'S A MAGAZINE CALLED *SPLOSH* THAT SOMEONE ONCE BOUGHT US FOR A JOKE. IT FEATURES NAKED WOMEN COVERED IN DIFFERENT TYPES OF FOOD. IT'S SILLY, BUT I ALSO FOUND IT KIND OF EROTIC AS AN IDEA, AND IT SPARKED OFF A FANTASY THAT INVOLVED ME COVERING MY PARTNER IN FRUIT AND PHOTOGRAPHING HER. IT WAS QUITE ARTISTIC WHEN WE DID IT: WE ARRANGED CHERRIES ON HER NIPPLES, AND HALF A MELON BETWEEN HER LEGS. THEN I ATE IT ALL OFF HER. I WOULDN'T DO IT ALL THE TIME BUT, NOW AND THEN, IT'S A REAL TURN-ON."

David, 34, Architect

Fantasies can be inspired by the stories and photo shoots in magazines. You and your lover can adopt the same poses and take instant photographs. (Keep them well hidden of course, just in case your relatives drop in unexpectedly.) The thrill of seeing yourself or your partner in a pornographic magazine-type pose will give you both the sexual excitement of posing "publicly," being seen as a sexual object, and, indulging in an activity often considered as "dirty."

DON'T FEEL THREATENED BY THE MODELS IN SOME MEN'S MAGAZINES. TAKE A GOOD LOOK AT THEM: OFTEN THEY ARE GIRL-NEXT-DOOR TYPES RATHER THAN STUNNINGLY BEAUTIFUL MODELS. REMEMBER THAT HE IS NOT INTERESTED IN THESE MODELS IN REAL LIFE—HE WANTS YOU!

CASE STUDY

"I WAS AMAZED WHEN MY GIRLFRIEND SAID SHE'D
LIKE TO LOOK AT ONE OF MY PORN MAGS. SHE
SAID THE PICTURES OF NAKED WOMEN TURNED
HER ON. SHE IMAGINED HERSELF IN THAT ROLE,
POSING FOR THE CAMERA, AND SHE EVEN
SUGGESTED WE ACTED OUT A FEW. WE DID
ONE WHERE SHE POSED ON A CHAIR,
STRADDLING IT LIKE THE GIRL IN THE MAG. THEN
SHE STARTED TO MASTURBATE. IT WAS THE
BIGGEST TURN-ON OF MY LIFE—AND SHE CAME AS
WELL, BECAUSE, SHE SAID SHE WAS IMAGINING
OTHER MEN GETTING HOT OVER HER PICTURE."

Bill, 34, Paramedic

A popular fantasy is of the photographer and porn model. You can act it out for real or just talk about the kind of pictures that you could take of each other, and this should be enough to get both of you feeling excited.

The magazines also feature stories. These stories are often very explicit, so if reading them aloud makes you too embarrassed then read them silently together. Use them to inspire suggestions for role-play and fantasies that you could act out for real.

Some couples like to take their fantasy of being desired by others to the point of sending in porn pictures of themselves for publication in a magazine. If you want to do this, check that your partner is happy, and remember that the magazine might be read by work colleagues, friends, or relatives.

You can borrow some of the raunchy language that porn magazines use. Try writing sexy notes to each other; outline what you'd like to do to your partner later in the day. Things that you'd never say are easier to write, and it can be a turn-on for both of you.

CASE STUDY

"I WRITE NOTES TO PAUL AND LEAVE THEM AROUND THE HOUSE, OR TUCKED INTO HIS BRIEFCASE. I SUGGEST SEXY THINGS I'D LIKE TO DO TO HIM. THEN, WHEN I KNOW HE MUST HAVE FOUND THEM, I FOLLOW THEM UP WITH TEXT MESSAGES. I FIND IT HARD TO TELL HIM THESE THINGS WHILE HE'S SITTING IN FRONT OF ME, SO USING MESSAGES TO SEDUCE HIM SLOWLY REALLY WORKS. I FIND I CAN EXPRESS MYSELF IN WAYS I'D NORMALLY SHY AWAY FROM."

Janna, 27, Producer

Using Camcorders

Filming yourselves on video while you are having sex is a real turn-on—whether it is a video of you acting out a fantasy, or just a film of you and your partner having raunchy sex that you can both fantasize over later on.

SET THE CAMERA ON A TRIPOD IF YOU WANT BOTH OF YOU IN THE SHOW. YOU MIGHT DO SOME TEST SHOTS TO ENSURE THAT THE POSITION THE CAMERA IS IN WILL ALLOW IT TO CATCH ALL THE ACTION.

ADD PROPS TO ENHANCE THE EROTIC ATMOSPHERE OF YOUR "BLUE MOVIE," SUCH AS A MIRRORS, A FEATHER BOA, HANDCUFFS, OR A WHIP. CHOOSE TOYS OR CLOTHING THAT WILL PUT YOU IN A PLAYFUL FRAME OF MIND.

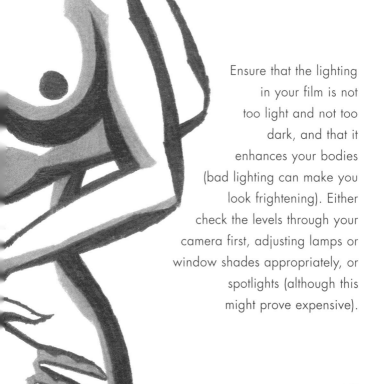

Ensure that the lighting in your film is not too light and not too dark, and that it enhances your bodies (bad lighting can make you look frightening). Either check the levels through your camera first, adjusting lamps or window shades appropriately, or spotlights (although this might prove expensive).

LOTS OF MOANS AND GASPS IN A HOME-MADE "BLUE MOVIE" WILL SOUND VERY SEXY WHEN YOU'RE FINALLY WATCHING IT, SO TRY TO SOUND AS EROTIC AS YOU LOOK. IF YOU LIKE, YOU CAN DUB SOME MUSIC OVER IT LATER.

You can write a script for a movie using specially prepared dialog or "scenes," between which you can change into different sexy outfits. The role-play ideas are endless— try a "business interview" that descends into wild sex, or even just "Sven, the repair man," who's come around to "fix the plumbing."

KEEP YOUR DIALOG SHORT (SO YOU DON'T FORGET IT OR BORE YOUR PARTNER), SUGGESTIVE, FUN, SEDUCTIVE, AND DON'T BE AFRAID TO USE THOSE SEXY PHRASES THAT YOU SEE IN PORN MAGS AND SOFT PORN BOOKS, SUCH AS, "OH SVEN, ARE YOU REALLY THE BEST PLUMBER IN TOWN?"

IF YOU FEEL UNCOMFORTABLE WITH SPEAKING, THEN DON'T—JUST MOAN AND GROAN AND SOUND SEXY.

CASE STUDY

"I ALWAYS FANTASIZED ABOUT BEING IN A PORN FILM, SO WHEN MY BOYFRIEND BOUGHT A NEW DIGITAL VIDEO CAMERA, I COULDN'T WAIT TO TRY IT OUT. WE RENTED A HOTEL ROOM BUT THE BEDROOM WASN'T SEXY ENOUGH. I DRESSED UP AS A BUSINESS TRAVELER. STEVE KNOCKED AT THE DOOR, PRETENDING TO HAVE ARRIVED FOR A MEETING. A FEW MINUTES LATER, WE WERE RIPPING EACH OTHER'S CLOTHES OFF. THE FILM WAS AMAZING— YOU COULD SEE EVERYTHING, BUT BECAUSE IT WAS US, IT DIDN'T FEEL SORDID AT ALL."

Lindsay, 31, Personal Assistant

CASE STUDY

"I LOVE TO FANTASIZE ABOUT MAKING PORN FILMS.
I THINK THAT IN REAL LIFE THEY'RE QUITE SAD, BUT IN
MY MIND I MAKE THESE FANTASTIC, ARTY MOVIES
WITH BEAUTIFUL WOMEN WHO ARE COMPLETELY IN
CONTROL. I THINK ABOUT THE SCRIPTS (A SORT OF
"COLD WAR SPY" LOOK IS CURRENTLY MY FAVORITE),
WHAT THEY'LL WEAR, AND EVEN HOW I'LL LIGHT IT.
I HAVE WHOLE STORIES IN MY HEAD, ENDING WITH
GORGEOUS MEN AND WOMEN HAVING SEX WITH
EACH OTHER, HALF-CLOTHED (WHICH IS SEXIER THAN
NAKED TO ME). I DON'T KNOW IF I'LL EVER DO IT BUT
IT'S A GREAT, ADAPTABLE BASIS FOR FANTASY."

Adam, 37, Photographer

The Internet

Since the advent of the Internet, the availability of pornography has been vastly increased. If you can pick your way through the less attractive sites, this can be good news for fantasy-lovers. Whatever your fantasy is, you can have it delivered to your screen in seconds.

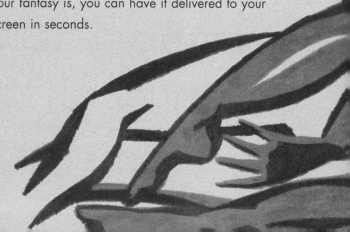

The Internet provides for all types of fantasies—
from S&M to masturbation. However, it can also be
a very solitary way of conducting your sex life. It
is not very easy to incorporate what happens
online into your lovemaking
and fantasy lives.

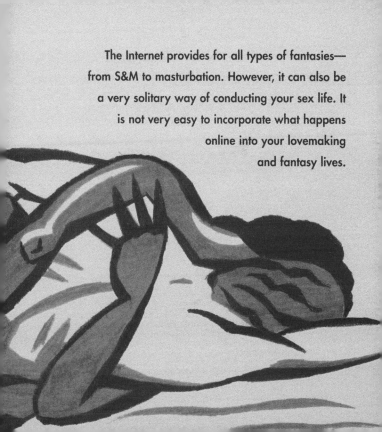

CASE STUDY

"I QUITE OFTEN LOG ON TO SOME OF THE
WEBCAM SITES. THE IMAGE IS A BIT FUZZY,
BUT THAT KIND OF ADDS TO THE THRILL. I
LIKE THE WHOLE SLEAZINESS OF IT, AND THE
IDEA THAT SOME WOMEN ARE TURNED ON
BY BEING ON THE WEB LIVE IS EXCITING. I
EXCHANGE MESSAGES WITH THEM
SOMETIMES; THE INTERACTION MAKES IT
LIKE PORN COME TO LIFE. I MAY NOT
WANT TO DO IT FOREVER, BUT RIGHT
NOW, WHILE I'M SINGLE, IT IS PERFECT."

Andy, 23, Executive

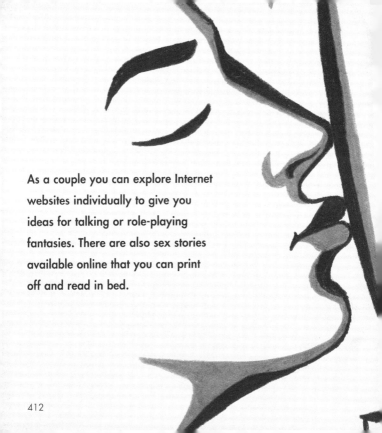

As a couple you can explore Internet websites individually to give you ideas for talking or role-playing fantasies. There are also sex stories available online that you can print off and read in bed.

As a couple, you and your lover might choose to log on to an Internet chatroom. You can use false names (you'll know these beforehand) and act out a fantasy online. If you enjoy a bit of exhibitionism, you might let other chat room members "listen in." Or, if you fancy a threesome, you might invite another chatroom member to join you!

CASE STUDY

"I ALWAYS WONDERED WHETHER I'D REALLY ENJOY A THREESOME, BECAUSE IT WAS OFTEN SOMETHING I'D FANTASIZED ABOUT. MY NEW PARTNER SHARED MY INTEREST FOR BOY-BOY-GIRL, BECAUSE HE LIKED THE IDEA OF WATCHING ME WITH ANOTHER MAN. SO WE POSTED AN AD IN A CHATROOM. WE INCLUDED A PHOTO OF ME IN LINGERIE. WE GOT LOTS OF REPLIES BUT I DIDN'T FEEL SAFE ENOUGH TO FOLLOW THEM UP IN THE END—THE RISK WAS JUST TOO BIG. I'D DO IT AGAIN BUT THIS TIME, I'D LOOK FOR A WOMAN. I'D FEEL SAFER THAT WAY."

Angie, 26, Waitress

YOU CAN ENJOY THE INTERNET ON YOUR OWN TO ENHANCE MASTURBATION THROUGH YOUR FANTASY. IF YOU LIKE TO MASTURBATE, AND YOU ENJOY FANTASY, THEN YOU'RE SURE TO FIND SOMETHING TO MEET YOUR NEEDS.

Using "cybersex," you can be anyone who you want to be. You can meet 'partners' online in chatrooms, and you can both enjoy fantasizing about who you are. It's always best to make it clear to the person you're "having sex" with that you are fantasizing, so that everyone knows what the situation is.

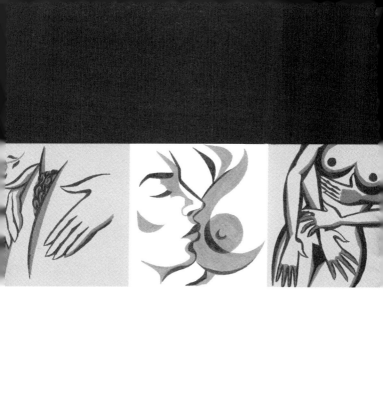

8 THOUGHTS ON FANTASY SEX

YOU CAN LET YOUR IMAGINATION RUN TO AS MANY DIFFERENT FANTASIES AS YOU ENJOY. YOU CAN USE WHAT MIGHT SEEM A BIT ODD TO OTHERS TO ENJOY BETTER LOVEMAKING.

Fantasy sex is the most fun you can have with your clothes on or off—because only in fantasy can you have a lesbian orgy, have sex with a gorilla, watch your partner strip for a cheering crowd, or take part in a virgin sacrifice...and you don't have to feel awkward about any of it.

"Sex is a body-contact sport. It is safe to watch but more fun to play."

Thomas Szasz, Sex by Prescription

Many couples' sex lives turn stale because they forget about playing, and put sex on a mental list of "things to do" underneath "buy toilet paper" and "clean out gutters." Sex slips to the bottom of the pile all too easily, and once you've lost the intimacy, that's when arguements begin.

SEXUAL PLAY WITH YOUR PARTNER CAN BEGIN AGAIN—IT JUST NEEDS A LITTLE INVESTMENT. YOU MUST SET ASIDE A TIME TO ENJOY BEING WITH EACH OTHER SEXUALLY, AND COMMIT YOURSELVES TO IT. THIS MIGHT SOUND FORCED, BUT IF YOU DON'T YOU'LL END UP SLUMPED IN FRONT OF THE TV AND SEX WILL NEVER HAPPEN. TAKE SOME TIME AND EXPERIMENT WITH YOUR FANTASIES.

CASE STUDY

"OUR SEX LIFE WAS NEARLY DEAD AND BURIED. THE ONLY FANTASY WE HAD WAS FOR THREE HOURS WITHOUT THE KIDS. BUT THEN WE BOOKED A WEEKEND AWAY AND DECIDED WE'D JUST DEDICATE IT TO SEX. WE PACKED SILLY COSTUMES— NURSE, MALE STRIPPER—HANDCUFFS, VIBRATORS, EVERYTHING! JUST DISCUSSING OUR SEXUAL FANTASIES TOGETHER WAS ENOUGH TO MAKE US HORNY. WE GOT INTO OUR ROOM AND WERE ALL OVER EACH OTHER. WE WERE AT IT NONSTOP ALL WEEKEND. IT REVITALIZED OUR SEX LIFE."

Connie, 34, Director

TOP TEN WAYS TO PLAY

1. SET ASIDE AN EARLY NIGHT ONCE A WEEK

2. BE PREPARED TO SHARE CERTAIN FANTASIES WITH YOUR PARTNER

3. WRITE DOWN YOUR FANTASIES AND SWAP THEM DURING THE DAY

4. INVEST IN SOME DRESSING-UP CLOTHES FOR SEXY CHARACTERS

5. TAKE A BOTTLE OF WINE TO BED TO LOOSEN YOUR INHIBITIONS

6. BLINDFOLD EACH OTHER AND DESCRIBE A SEXUAL SCENARIO

7. PLAY STRIP POKER, WITH FORFEITS THAT INCLUDE DISCUSSING FANTASIES

8. READ EROTIC LITERATURE TO EACH OTHER

9. GO AWAY FOR THE NIGHT TO A DIFFERENT ENVIRONMENT

10. RENT A SEXY VIDEO, AND WATCH IT TOGETHER. THEN ACT OUT SCENES FROM IT.

> "I like men who have a future
> and women who have a past."
>
> Oscar Wilde, The Picture of Dorian Gray

It's still true that many men are insecure about their partner's past. Women can be too, but unfortunately men tend to be a little more paranoid about other men that their partner slept with before him—based on whether they had bigger penises, whether they were better in bed, whether she had more orgasms.

If you must fantasize about the past, at the very least, don't confess.

SHARING FANTASIES ABOUT EXES IS A
VERY DANGEROUS PATH TO TREAD.
UNLESS BOTH PARTNERS ARE SO SECURE
IN THE CURRENT RELATIONSHIP THAT
JEALOUSY PLAYS NO PART WHATSOEVER,
IT'S LIKELY THAT EVEN BRINGING UP THE
TOPIC OF PREVIOUS PARTNERS WILL BE
FRAUGHT WITH DANGER.

CASE STUDY

"I NEVER ASK ABOUT DAVID'S PAST AND HE NEVER ASKS ABOUT MINE. BUT WE DO TALK ABOUT WHO WE FANCY IN THE MOVIES. I DON'T MIND HEARING ABOUT HOW HE'D LOVE TO HAVE SEX WITH AN ACTRESS, BECAUSE I AM HIS REALITY AND HE'S HARDLY GOING TO LEAVE ME FOR JULIA ROBERTS. I CAN ALSO TELL HIM ABOUT SCENES IN MOVIES THAT TURN ME ON, OR ACTORS THAT REALLY DO IT FOR ME. A YOUNG PAUL NEWMAN IS MY IDEAL, AND SOMETIMES DAVE WILL TELL ME TO SHUT MY EYES AND PRETEND HE IS HIM. IT'S JUST FOR FUN, AND IF EITHER OF US FELT INSECURE WE'D STOP."

Alice, 27, Accounts Manager

"Is it not strange that desire should so many years outlive performance?"

William Shakespeare

The beauty of fantasy is that age is no barrier to good sex. Even if your chandelier-swinging years were over and done with long ago, you can still fantasize all you like about hurtling through the air naked on the flying trapeze, or rendering men speechless with desire for your stunning, youthful body.

Fantasy is even more important as we age, because it allows us to remain sexual beings, even when things have changed physically. After divorce, or even widowhood, it's still important to view oneself as sexually active. You can be single for years but maintain a healthy, sensual side to your life with fantasy and masturbation.

CASE STUDY

"I'VE BEEN SINGLE FOR THREE YEARS SINCE DIVORCE, BUT I HAVE YOUNG KIDS AT HOME. I DON'T WANT TO GO AROUND JUST PICKING UP WOMEN FOR SEX, SO I FANTASIZE INSTEAD. I HAVE A FERTILE IMAGINATION, AND DAYDREAM ABOUT WOMEN I'VE SEEN AND FANCIED, OR ABOUT EX-GIRLFRIENDS. MY FANTASIES AREN'T OUTRAGEOUS—A BLOW-JOB IS USUALLY AS FAR AS IT GOES. IT HELPS ME TO REMEMBER MY SEX LIFE HASN'T REACHED THE END OF THE ROAD, IT'S JUST A TEMPORARY BLIP. I FEEL ENERGIZED AND HAPPY AFTER I'VE MASTURBATED OVER A GOOD, LIFE-AFFIRMING FANTASY."

Barry, 38, Driver

"As she lay there dozing next to me, one voice inside my head kept saying, 'Relax... you are not the first doctor to sleep with one of his patients,' but another kept reminding me, 'Howard, you are a veterinarian.'"

from a novel by Dick Wilson

HOWEVER SEEMINGLY STRANGE YOUR
FANTASY, IF IT'S HAPPENING IN YOUR HEAD
—AND NOT ON MAIN STREET—IT'S OK.

Nancy Friday's famous books of women's
and men's fantasies (*My Secret Garden*,
Forbidden Flowers, *Men In Love*, and
Women on Top) detail fantasies you
couldn't imagine your friendly neighbor or
buttoned-up boss enjoying. But they do.

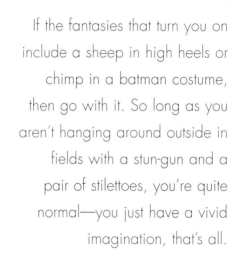

If the fantasies that turn you on include a sheep in high heels or chimp in a batman costume, then go with it. So long as you aren't hanging around outside in fields with a stun-gun and a pair of stilettoes, you're quite normal—you just have a vivid imagination, that's all.

TOP ALTERNATIVE
FANTASY PARTNERS

1. DOGS

2. HORSES

3. MONKEYS

4. SNAKES

5. TIGERS AND LIONS

6. CARTOON CHARACTERS, LIKE JESSICA RABBIT

7. ETHEREAL BEINGS, LIKE ANGELS OR GHOSTS

8. ALIENS

9. HISTORICAL FIGURES, LIKE GEORGE WASHINGTON

10. MYTHICAL CREATURES, SUCH AS GIANTS

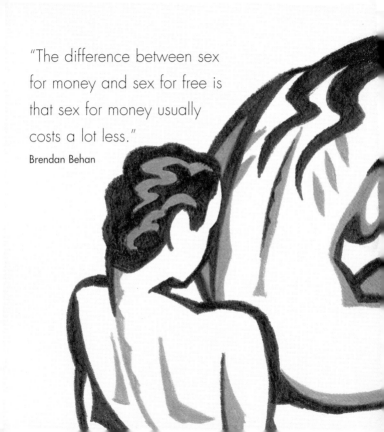

"The difference between sex for money and sex for free is that sex for money usually costs a lot less."
Brendan Behan

Sex for money is a staple of male and female fantasy, mainly because it removes the emotional complications of sex with a partner and replaces them with a physical transaction. While in real life the exchange may be demeaning or depressing, in fantasy, it allows the participants to be as sexual as they like, without inhibition.

Sex in exchange for money is a staple of books, TV, and films, such as *Indecent Proposal*, because people will always pay for no-strings-attached sex. Between partners, however, it can be a rewarding fantasy that allows them to explore every side of their sexuality without guilt.

449

CASE STUDY

"I FANTASIZE ABOUT BEING A PROSTITUTE. BEING
PAID MEANS I DON'T HAVE TO MAKE DECISIONS,
OR WORRY ABOUT HOW I APPEAR. I IMAGINE
MANY CUSTOMERS WHO ALL WANT
DIFFERENT SERVICES—IT CAN GET VERY KINKY.
MY FAVORITE IS WHEN I SIT ON A CLIENT IN
A CAR AND SCREW HIM, FAST. HE THEN
PAYS ME AND LEAVES. I KNOW I'D HATE IT
IN REALITY, BUT THE FANTASY MAKES ME
FEEL POWERFUL AND SEXY."

Megan, 29, Supervisor

450

"Lifelong committed sex has the potential to be more thrilling, more varied, more satisfying in every way than any other sexual arrangement you can think of."

Dagmar O'Connor, *How to Make Love to the Same Person For the Rest of Your Life*

This may well be true, but it's hard to achieve. But fantasy can be the glue that keeps you together sexually. Within fantasy you can enjoy a thousand different partners: six at a time or one by one. You can make love to movie stars, ex-partners, or even friends.

SOME OF YOUR FANTASIES WILL INVOLVE YOUR PARTNER AND SOME WON'T—YOU CAN DECIDE WHETHER TO TELL THEM. THE LONGER YOU KNOW YOUR PARTNER, AND THE MORE BONDED YOU BECOME SEXUALLY, THE MORE YOU'LL WANT TO SHARE YOUR FANTASIES WITH THEM. ROLE-PLAY, DISCUSSING FANTASIES, AND DRESSING UP CAN ALL KEEP YOUR SEX LIFE HOT FOR YEARS. THE MORE OPEN YOU ARE TO FANTASY, THE MORE LIKELY IT IS THAT YOU'LL STAY TOGETHER FOREVER.

455

"There is nothing wrong with going to bed with someone of your own sex…. People should be very free with sex, they should draw the line at goats."

Elton John

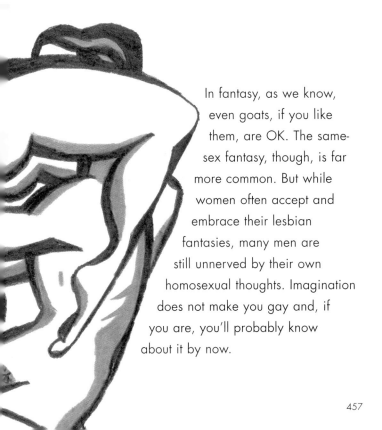

In fantasy, as we know, even goats, if you like them, are OK. The same-sex fantasy, though, is far more common. But while women often accept and embrace their lesbian fantasies, many men are still unnerved by their own homosexual thoughts. Imagination does not make you gay and, if you are, you'll probably know about it by now.

IF THE IDEA OF SEX WITH SOMEONE OF YOUR
GENDER TURNS YOU ON, WHY FIGHT IT? SOME
PEOPLE PUT THE FANTASY INTO REALITY WITH
THREESOMES. HOWEVER, A THREESOME CAN
ONLY WORK IN PRACTICE FOR SOME. IF FANTASY
IS AS FAR AS YOU'RE PREPARED TO GO, LET
YOURSELF EXPLORE THIS SIDE OF YOUR SEXUALITY IN
YOUR OWN WAY, WITHOUT ANY GUILT.

TOP 10 SAME-SEX FANTASIES

1. TWO WOMEN TOGETHER, MAN WATCHING

2. TWO WOMEN ALONE TOGETHER

3. TWO MEN TOGETHER, WOMAN WATCHING

4. TWO MEN ALONE TOGETHER

5. TWO WOMEN AND A MAN TOGETHER

6. TWO MEN AND A WOMAN TOGETHER

7. A LESBIAN ORGY

8. A GAY ORGY

9. MAN BEING SEDUCED BY A MAN

10. WOMAN BEING SEDUCED BY A WOMAN

Sadism and masochism are also highly popular fantasies, and, while many might hesitate to put the dom–sub principles into practice, the idea can be highly erotic. Luckily, dominance and submission is a sexual practice that can be flirted with without going all the way into S&M. In role-play, a little light bondage or "sex-slavery" can be a turn-on without any actual pain. And in your mind, you can enjoy experiences that physically would be impossible.

Rubber, PVC, or leather are all suggestive of dominance and submission. In role-play, you can whip, tie, or tease each other. If you do go further into the realms of pain, though, be very careful, because fantasy doesn't always translate into reality.

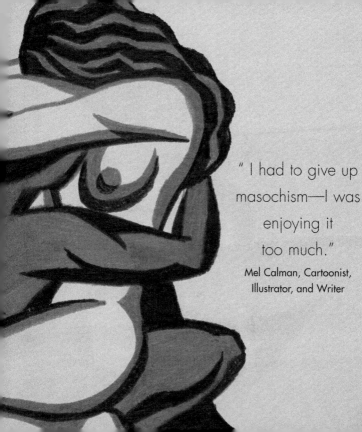

" I had to give up masochism—I was enjoying it too much."

Mel Calman, Cartoonist, Illustrator, and Writer

CASE STUDY

"I HAVE ALWAYS BEEN TURNED ON BY THE IDEA OF S&M, AND SO HAS MY GIRLFRIEND. WE HAVE TRIED WHIPS AND TYING EACH OTHER UP. WE WHISPER IDEAS TO EACH OTHER DURING SEX, ABOUT BONDAGE AND CLOTHING. EVEN IF I HOLD HER HANDS ABOVE HER HEAD IT TURNS HER ON. SHE ONCE CONFESSED THAT SHE WAS IMAGINING BEING TIED UP IN FRONT OF A ROOM FULL OF YOUNG NOVICE MONKS, ALL OF WHOM WERE DESPERATE TO TOUCH HER!"

Tom, 30, Gardener.

Published by MQ Publications Limited
12 The Ivories, 6–8 Northampton Street
London N1 2HY
Tel: 020 7359 2244   Fax: 020 7359 1616
email: mail@mqpublications.com

Text © Flic Everett 2002
Design: Flora Awolaja
Illustrations: Alan Adler

ISBN: 1-84072-419-6

1 3 5 7 9 0 8 6 4 2

Printed and bound in Hong Kong